Godot Engine Game Development Projects

Build five cross-platform 2D and 3D games with Godot 3.0

Chris Bradfield

BIRMINGHAM - MUMBAI

Godot Engine Game Development Projects

Acquisition Editor: Nigel Fernandes
Content Development Editor: Jason Pereira
Technical Editor: Rutuja Vaze
Copy Editor: Safis Editing
Project Coordinator: Sheejal Shah
Proofreader: Safis Editing
Indexer: Mariammal Chettiyar
Graphics: Disha Haria
Production Coordinator: Shraddha Falebhai

First published: June 2018

Production reference: 1270618

Published by Packt Publishing Ltd.
Livery Place
35 Livery Street
Birmingham
B3 2PB, UK.

ISBN 978-1-78883-150-5

www.packtpub.com

To my son, Damian, and my daughter, Nadia, for being a constant source of love and pride.
To Priya for being a wonderful wife and mother.

`mapt.io`

Mapt is an online digital library that gives you full access to over 5,000 books and videos, as well as industry leading tools to help you plan your personal development and advance your career. For more information, please visit our website.

Why subscribe?

- Spend less time learning and more time coding with practical eBooks and Videos from over 4,000 industry professionals

- Improve your learning with Skill Plans built especially for you

- Get a free eBook or video every month

- Mapt is fully searchable

- Copy and paste, print, and bookmark content

PacktPub.com

Did you know that Packt offers eBook versions of every book published, with PDF and ePub files available? You can upgrade to the eBook version at `www.PacktPub.com` and as a print book customer, you are entitled to a discount on the eBook copy. Get in touch with us at `service@packtpub.com` for more details.

At `www.PacktPub.com`, you can also read a collection of free technical articles, sign up for a range of free newsletters, and receive exclusive discounts and offers on Packt books and eBooks.

Foreword

In December 2014, Godot Engine 1.0 was released. With this first public release, the feature-packed, free, and open source project delivered on its promise of a cross-platform, easy-to-use, and powerful game creation tool.

I fell in love with Godot's high-level features and its permissive license, so I jumped right in, with no prior game development experience. I felt a bit lost when I first opened the editor. I moved on to the online documentation and started reading the well-written, step-by-step introduction. It covered basic concepts, such as scenes and nodes and the GDScript programming language, and it showed how to create a Pong clone, and that was basically it, at that time. There were some more tutorials on advanced features, but there was a gap between them and the first guide. As a complete beginner, I was stuck with the following question: how do I make my first game? Yet, I kept exploring, and with the help of the Godot community, I could eventually build a simple 2D game with a local multiplayer. What a feeling to see your first game on the screen!

Fast-forward to 3 years from then, Godot has grown a lot as a project, a community, and an engine. Godot 3.0 was released in January 2018 after 18 months of work. It brought this free, community-driven project to the level of its proprietary counterparts for 2D and 3D game development. The beginner game developer that I was became a project manager, helping to organize and focus the work of hundreds of contributors revolving around the engine. Working together with people from all around the world improved all areas of the project: engine features, usability, localization, and, of course, documentation.
Thanks to many dedicated contributors, Godot's documentation became one of the most accessible technical resources that I have seen in free and open source projects. This is in great part thanks to Chris Bradfield, the author of this book, who spent countless hours writing new material and reviewing contributions to ensure their accuracy and quality of writing.

With this book, Chris goes one step further and provides a thorough answer to that question (how do I make my first game?), shared by many Godot beginners. Indeed, he goes beyond that, as Godot Engine Game Development Projects will lead you through the creation of five full-featured games—four in 2D and one in 3D. Each game introduces new features and concepts of Godot so that you can learn how and when to use them in your own creations. Advanced users with experience in other game development tools (or even Godot itself) will learn how to use Godot's unique architecture and features to write better, more maintainable code through Chris' showcase of best practices.

From setting up Godot for the first time on your computer to publishing your own games to a wide range of platforms, Chris runs you through all the steps in a concise yet thorough way. After the first lesson, you should already be able to see how straightforward and accessible game development can be with a tool such as Godot, even if you had no prior experience in game creation. You will also feel a great sense of accomplishment seeing your own creation playing on your computer or smartphone, with the power to implement new gameplay elements with just a few lines of code.

I wish you a lot of fun on your game development journey, and a warm welcome to the Godot community.

Rémi Verschelde

Godot Engine – Project Manager

Contributors

About the author

Chris Bradfield has been working in the internet technology space for more than 25 years. He has worked in the online gaming space for a number of successful MMOs and social gaming publishers in South Korea and the United States. Throughout his game industry career, he has served as a game designer, developer, product manager, and business development executive.

In 2012, he discovered his love for teaching and founded KidsCanCode to provide programming instruction and curriculum to middle and high school students. He is also a member of the Godot Engine documentation team and works to provide learning resources for game development students around the world.

I would like to expresses my gratitude to Sokoban Pack by Kenney Vleugels, Spaceship art founder skorpio, Sunny Land art by Luis Zuno (@ansimuz), and 3D Minigolf tiles by YeOldeDM for their work.

About the reviewer

Max Hilbrunner is a Godot Engine contributor and CTO at aiPhilos and works on providing better product search experiences using artificial intelligence, natural language processing, and machine learning in cooperation with the **German Research Center for Artificial Intelligence (DFKI)**.

Packt is searching for authors like you

If you're interested in becoming an author for Packt, please visit `authors.packtpub.com` and apply today. We have worked with thousands of developers and tech professionals, just like you, to help them share their insight with the global tech community. You can make a general application, apply for a specific hot topic that we are recruiting an author for, or submit your own idea.

Table of Contents

Preface

This book is an introduction to the Godot game engine and its new version, 3.0. Godot 3.0 has a large number of new features and capabilities that make it a strong alternative to more expensive commercial game engines. For beginners, it offers a friendly way to learn game development techniques. For more experienced developers, Godot is a powerful, customizable tool for bringing visions to life.

This book will have a project-based approach. It consists of five projects that will help developers achieve a sound understanding of how to use the Godot engine to build games.

Who this book is for

This book is for anyone who wants to learn how to make games using a modern game engine. New users and experienced developers alike will find it a helpful resource. Some programming experience is recommended.

What this book covers

This book is a project-based introduction to using the Godot game engine. Each of the five game projects builds on the concepts learned in the previous project.

Chapter 1, *Introduction*, introduces the concept of game engines in general and Godot specifically, including how to download Godot and install it on your computer.

Chapter 2, *Coin Dash*, deals with a small game that demonstrates how to create scenes and work with Godot's node architecture.

Chapter 3, *Escape the Maze*, entails a project based on a top-down maze game that will show how to use Godot's powerful inheritance features and nodes for tile maps and sprite animation.

Chapter 4, *Space Rocks*, demonstrates working with physics bodies to create an *Asteroids*-style space game.

Chapter 5, *Jungle Jump*, involves a side-scrolling platform game in the spirit of *Super Mario Brothers*. You'll learn about kinematic bodies, animation states, and parallax backgrounds.

Chapter 6, *3D Minigolf*, extends the previous concepts into three dimensions. You'll work with meshes, lighting, and camera control.

Chapter 7, *Additional Topics*, covers even more topics to explore once you've mastered the material in the previous chapters.

To get the most out of this book

To best understand the example code in this book, you should have a general knowledge of programming, preferably with a modern, dynamically-typed language, such as Python or JavaScript. If you're new to programming entirely, you may wish to review a beginner Python tutorial before diving into the game projects in this book.

Godot will run on any relatively modern PC running Windows, macOS, or Linux operating systems. Your video card must support OpenGL ES 3.0.

Download the example code files

You can download the example code files for this book from your account at www.packtpub.com. If you purchased this book elsewhere, you can visit www.packtpub.com/support and register to have the files emailed directly to you.

You can download the code files by following these steps:

1. Log in or register at www.packtpub.com.
2. Select the **SUPPORT** tab.
3. Click on **Code Downloads & Errata**.
4. Enter the name of the book in the **Search** box and follow the onscreen instructions.

Once the file is downloaded, please make sure that you unzip or extract the folder using the latest version of:

- WinRAR/7-Zip for Windows
- Zipeg/iZip/UnRarX for Mac
- 7-Zip/PeaZip for Linux

The code bundle for the book is also hosted on GitHub at https://github.com/ PacktPublishing/Godot-Game-Engine-Projects/issues. In case there's an update to the code, it will be updated on the existing GitHub repository.

We also have other code bundles from our rich catalog of books and videos available at https://github.com/PacktPublishing/. Check them out!

Download the color images

We also provide a PDF file that has color images of the screenshots/diagrams used in this book. You can download it here: https://www.packtpub.com/sites/default/files/downloads/GodotEngineGameDevelopmentProjects_ColorImages.pdf.

Conventions used

There are a number of text conventions used throughout this book.

CodeInText: Indicates code words in text, database table names, folder names, filenames, file extensions, pathnames, dummy URLs, user input, and Twitter handles. Here is an example: "Mount the downloaded WebStorm-10*.dmg disk image file as another disk in your system."

A block of code is set as follows:

```
extends Area2D

export (int) var speed
var velocity = Vector2()
var screensize = Vector2(480, 720)
```

Any command-line input or output is written as follows:

```
adb install dodge.apk
```

Bold: Indicates a new term, an important word, or words that you see onscreen. For example, words in menus or dialog boxes appear in the text like this. Here is an example: "The main portion of the editor window is the **Viewport**."

 Warnings or important notes appear like this.

 Tips and tricks appear like this.

Get in touch

Feedback from our readers is always welcome.

General feedback: Email `feedback@packtpub.com` and mention the book title in the subject of your message. If you have questions about any aspect of this book, please email us at `questions@packtpub.com`.

Errata: Although we have taken every care to ensure the accuracy of our content, mistakes do happen. If you have found a mistake in this book, we would be grateful if you would report this to us. Please visit `www.packtpub.com/submit-errata`, selecting your book, clicking on the Errata Submission Form link, and entering the details.

Piracy: If you come across any illegal copies of our works in any form on the Internet, we would be grateful if you would provide us with the location address or website name. Please contact us at `copyright@packtpub.com` with a link to the material.

If you are interested in becoming an author: If there is a topic that you have expertise in and you are interested in either writing or contributing to a book, please visit `authors.packtpub.com`.

Reviews

Please leave a review. Once you have read and used this book, why not leave a review on the site that you purchased it from? Potential readers can then see and use your unbiased opinion to make purchase decisions, we at Packt can understand what you think about our products, and our authors can see your feedback on their book. Thank you!

For more information about Packt, please visit `packtpub.com`.

Introduction 1

Whether it's your desired career or a recreational hobby, game development is a fun and rewarding endeavor. There never been a better time to get started in game development. Modern programming languages and tools have made it easier than ever to build high-quality games and distribute them to the world. If you're reading this book, then you've set your feet on the path to making the game of your dreams.

This book is an introduction to the Godot game engine and its new 3.0 version, which was released in early 2018. Godot 3.0 has a large number of new features and capabilities that make it a strong alternative to expensive commercial game engines. For beginners, it offers a friendly way to learn fundamental game development techniques. For more experienced developers, Godot is a powerful, customizable, and *open* tool for bringing your visions to life.

This book takes a project-based approach that will introduce you to the fundamentals of the engine. It consists of five games that are designed to help you achieve a sound understanding of game development concepts and how they're applied in Godot. Along the way, you will learn how Godot works and absorb important techniques that you can apply to your projects.

General advice

This section contains some general advice to readers, based on the author's experience as a teacher and lecturer. Keep these tips in mind as you work through the book, especially if you're very new to programming.

Try to follow the projects in the book in order. Later chapters may build on topics that were introduced in earlier chapters, where they are explained in more detail. When you encounter something that you don't remember, go back and review that topic in the earlier chapter. No one is timing you, and there's no prize for finishing the book quickly.

There is a lot of material to absorb here. Don't feel discouraged if you don't get it at first. The goal is not to become an expert in game development overnight—that's just not possible. Repetition is the key to learning complex topics; the more you work with Godot's features, the more familiar and *easy* they will start to seem. Try looking back at `Chapter 2`, *Coin Dash*, when you finish `Chapter 7`, *Additional Topics*. You'll be surprised at how much more you'll understand compared to the first time you read it.

If you're using the PDF version of this book, resist the temptation to copy and paste the code. Typing the code yourself will engage more of your brain. It's similar to how taking notes during a lecture helps you learn better than just listening, even if you never read the notes. If you're a slow typist, it will also help you work on your typing speed. In a nutshell: you're a programmer, so get used to typing code!

One of the biggest mistakes that new game developers make is taking on a bigger project than they can handle. It is very important to keep the scope of your project as small as possible when starting out. You will be much more successful (and learn more) if you finish two or three small games than if you have a large, incomplete project that has grown beyond your ability to manage.

You'll notice that the five games in this book follow this strategy very strictly. They are all small in scope, both for practical reasons—to fit reasonably into book-sized lessons—but also to remain focused on teaching you the basics. As you build them, you will likely find yourself thinking of additional features and gameplay elements right away. *What if the spaceship had upgrades? What if the character could do wall jumps?*

Ideas are great, but if you haven't finished the basic project yet, write them down and save them for later. Don't let yourself be sidetracked by one *cool idea* after another. Developers call this *feature creep*, and it's a trap that has led to many an unfinished game. Don't fall victim to it.

Finally, don't forget to take a break now and again. You shouldn't try and power through the whole book in just a few sittings. After each new concept, and especially after each chapter, give yourself time to absorb the new information before you dive into the next one. You'll find that you not only retain more information, but you'll probably enjoy the process more.

What is a game engine?

Game development is complex and involves a wide variety of knowledge and skills. In order to build a modern game, you need a great deal of underlying technology before you can make the actual game itself. Imagine that you had to build your own computer and write your own operating system before you could even start programming. Game development would be a lot like that if you truly had to start from scratch and build *everything* you needed.

In addition, there are a number of common needs that every game has. For example, no matter what the game is, it's going to need to draw things on the screen. If the code to do that has already been written, it makes more sense to reuse it than to create it all over again for every game. That's where game frameworks and engines come in.

A **game framework** is a set of libraries with helper code that assists in building the foundational parts of a game. It doesn't necessarily provide all the pieces, and you may still have to write a great deal of code to tie everything together. Because of this, building a game with a game framework can take more time than one built with a full game engine.

A **game engine** is a collection of tools and technologies designed to ease the process of game-making by removing the need to *reinvent the wheel* for each new game project. It provides a framework of commonly needed functionality that often needs a significant investment in time to develop.

Here is a list of some of the main features a game engine will provide:

- **Rendering (2D and 3D)**: Rendering is the process of displaying your game on the player's screen. A good rendering pipeline must take into account modern GPU support, high-resolution displays, and effects like lighting, perspective, and viewports, while maintaining a very high frame rate.
- **Physics**: While a very common requirement, building a robust and accurate physics engine is a monumental task. Most games require some sort of collision detection and response system, and many need physics simulation, but few developers want to take on the task of writing one, especially if they have ever tried to do so.
- **Platform support**: In today's market, most developers want to be able to release their games on multiple platforms, such as consoles, mobile, PC, and/or the web. A game engine provides a unified exporting process to publish on multiple platforms without needing to rewrite game code or support multiple versions.

- **Common development environment**: By using the same unified interface to make multiple games, you don't have to re learn a new workflow every time you start a new project.

In addition, there will be tools to assist with features such as networking, easing the process of working with images and sound, animations, debugging, level creation, and many more. Often, game engines will include the ability to import content from other tools such as those used to create animations or 3D models.

Using a game engine allows the developer to focus on building their game, rather than creating all of the underlying framework needed to make it work. For small or independent developers, this can mean the difference between releasing a game after one year of development instead of three, or even never at all.

There are dozens of popular game engines on the market today, such as Unity, Unreal Engine, and GameMaker Studio, just to name a few. An important fact to be aware of is that the majority of popular game engines are commercial products. They may or may not require any financial investment to get started, but they will require some kind of licensing and/or royalty payments if your game makes money. Whatever engine you choose, you need to carefully read the user agreement and make sure you understand what you are and are not allowed to with the engine, and what hidden costs, if any, you may be responsible for.

On the other hand, there are some engines which are non-commercial and *open source*, such as the Godot game engine, which is what this book is all about.

What is Godot?

Godot is a fully featured modern game engine, providing all of the features described in the previous section and more. It is also completely free and open source, released under the very permissive MIT license. This means there are no fees, no hidden costs, and no royalties to pay on your game's revenue. Everything you make with Godot 100% belongs to you, which is not the case with many commercial game engines that require an ongoing contractual relationship. For many developers, this is very appealing.

If you're not familiar with the concept of open source, community-driven development, this may seem strange to you. However, much like the Linux kernel, Firefox browser, and many other very well-known pieces of software, Godot is not developed by a company as a commercial product. Instead, a dedicated community of passionate developers donate their time and expertise to building the engine, testing and fixing bugs, producing documentation, and more.

As a game developer, the benefits of using Godot are vast. Because it is unencumbered by commercial licensing, you have complete control over exactly how and where your game is distributed. Many commercial game engines restrict the types of projects you can make, or require a much more expensive license to build games in certain categories, such as gambling.

Godot's open source nature also means there is a level of transparency that doesn't exist with commercial game engines. For example, if you find that a particular engine feature doesn't quite meet your needs, you are free to modify the engine itself and add the new features you need, no permission required. This can also be very helpful when debugging a large project, because you have full access to the engine's internal workings.

It also means that you can directly contribute to Godot's future. See `Chapter 7`, *Additional Topics*, for more information about how you can get involved with Godot development.

Downloading Godot

You can download the latest version of Godot by visiting `https://godotengine.org/` and clicking **Download**. This book is written for version 3.0. If the version you download has another number at the end (like 3.0.3), that's fine—this just means that it includes updates to version 3.0 that fix bugs or other issues.

 A version 3.1 release is currently in development and may have been released by the time you read this book. This version may or may not include changes that are incompatible with the code in this book. Check the GitHub repository for this book for information and errata: `https://github.com/PacktPublishing/Godot-Game-Engine-Projects`

On the download page, there are a few options that bear explaining. First, 32-bit versus 64-bit: this option depends on your operating system and your computer's processor. If you're not sure, you should choose the 64-bit version. You will also see a *Mono Version*. This is a version specially built to be used with the C# programming language. Don't download this one unless you plan to use C# with Godot. At the time of writing, C# support is still experimental, and is not recommended for beginners.

Double-click on the file you downloaded to unzip it, and you'll have the Godot application. Optionally, you can drag it to your `Programs` or `Applications` folder, if you have one. Double-click the application to launch it and you'll see Godot's **Project Manager** window.

Alternate installation methods

There are a few other ways to get Godot on your computer besides downloading it from the Godot website. Note that there is no difference in functionality when installed this way. The following are merely alternatives for downloading the application:

- **Steam**: If you have an account on Steam, you can install Godot via the Steam desktop application. Search for Godot in the Steam store and follow the instructions to install it. You can launch Godot from the Steam application and it will even track your *playtime*.

- **Package Managers**: If you're using one of the following operating system package managers, you can install Godot via its normal install process. See the documentation for your package manager for details. Godot is available in these package managers:
  - Homebrew (macOS)
  - Scoop (Windows)
  - Snap (Linux)

Overview of the Godot UI

Like most game engines, Godot has a unified development environment. This means that you use the same interface to work on all of the aspects of your game—code, visuals, audio, and so on. This section is an introduction to the interface and its parts. Take note of the terminology used here; it will be used throughout this book when referring to actions you'll take in the editor window.

Project Manager

The **Project Manager** is the first window you'll see when you open Godot:

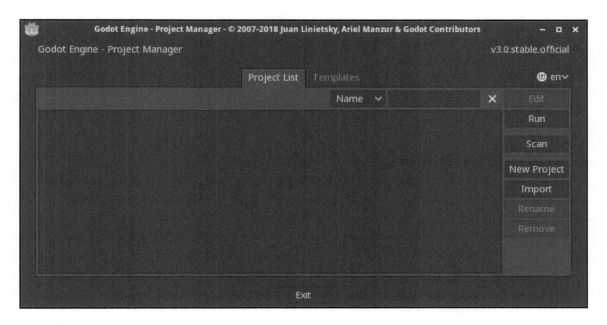

In this window, you can see a list of your existing Godot projects. You can choose an existing project and click **Run** to play the game or click **Edit** to work on it in the Godot Editor (refer to the following screenshot). You can also create a new project by clicking **New Project**:

Here, you can give the project a name and create a folder to store it in. Always try to choose a name that describes the project. Also keep in mind that different operating systems handle capitalization and spaces in filenames differently. It's a good idea to stick to lowercase and use underscores, _, instead of spaces for maximum compatibility.

Note the warning message—in Godot, each project is stored as a separate folder on the computer. All the files that the project uses are in this folder. Nothing outside of this project folder will be accessible in the game, so you need to put any images, sounds, models, or other data into the project folder. This makes it convenient to share Godot projects; you only need to zip the project folder and you can be confident that another Godot user will be able to open it and not be missing any necessary data.

Choosing filenames

When you're naming your new project, there are a few simple rules you should try and follow that may save you some trouble in the future. Give your project a name that describes what it is—*Wizard Battle Arena* is a much better project name than *Game #2*. In the future, you'll never be able to remember which game #2 was, so be as descriptive as possible.

You should also think about how you name your project folder and the files in it. Some operating systems are *case-sensitive* and distinguish between `My_Game` and `my_game`, while others do not. This can lead to problems if you move your project from one computer to another. For this reason, many programmers develop a standardized naming scheme for their projects, for example: *No spaces in filenames, use "_" between words*. Regardless of what naming scheme you adopt, the most important thing is to be consistent.

Once you've created the project folder, the **Create & Edit** button will open the new project in the **Editor** window.

Try it now: create a project called `test_project`.

 If you're using a version of the Windows operating system, you'll also see a console window open when you run Godot. In this window, you can see warnings and errors produced by the engine and/or your project. This window doesn't appear under macOS or Linux, but you can see the console output if you launch the application from the command line using a Terminal program.

Editor window

The following is a screenshot of the main Godot editor window. This is where you will spend most of your time when building projects in Godot. The editor interface is divided into several sections, each offering different functionality. The specific terminology for each section is described as follows:

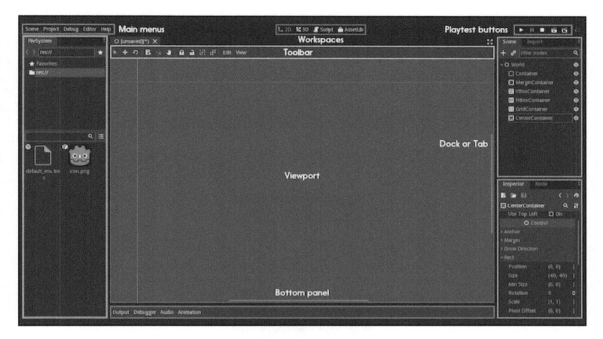

Godot Editor Window

The main portion of the editor window is the **Viewport**. This is where you'll see parts of your game as you're working on them.

In the upper-left corner is the Main menus, where you can save and load files, edit project settings, and get help.

In the center at the top is a list of the Workspaces you can switch between when working on different parts of your game. You can switch between **2D** and **3D** mode, as well **Script** mode, where you can edit your game's code. The **AssetLib** is a place where you can download add-ons and example projects. See Chapter 7, *Additional Topics*, for more information on using the **AssetLib**. Refer to the following screenshot:

The following screenshot shows the Workspaces buttons on the toolbar. The icons in the toolbar will change based on what kind of object you are editing. So will the items in the Bottom panel, which will open various smaller windows for accessing specific information such as debugging, audio settings, and more:

The buttons in the upper-right Playtest area are for launching the game and interacting with it when it's running:

Finally, on the left and right sides are the Docks you can use to view and select game items and set their properties. The left-hand dock contains the **FileSystem** tab:

All of the files inside the project folder are shown here, and you can click on folders to open them and see what they contain. All resources in your project will be located relative to `res://`, which is the project's root folder. For example, a file path might look like this: `res://player/Player.tscn`.

In the right-hand dock, you can see several tabs. The **Scene** tab shows the current scene you are working on in the Viewport. In the **Inspector** tab below it, you can see and adjust the properties of any object you select. Refer to the following screenshot:

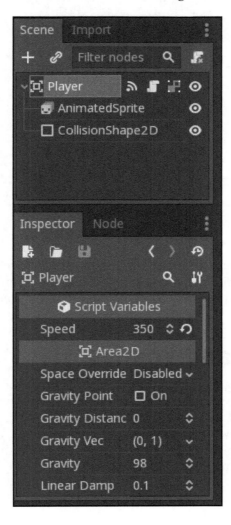

Selecting the **Import** tab and clicking on a file in the **FileSystem** tab lets you adjust how Godot imports resources like textures, meshes, and sounds, as shown in the following screenshot:

As you work through the game projects in this book, you'll learn about the functionality of these items and become familiar with navigating the editor interface. However, there are a few other concepts you need to know about before getting started.

About nodes and scenes

Nodes are the basic building blocks for creating games in Godot. A node is an object that can represent a variety of specialized game functions. A given type of node might display graphics, play an animation, or represent a 3D model of an object. The node also contains a collection of properties, allowing you to customize its behavior. Which nodes you add to your project depends on what functionality you need. It's a modular system designed to give you flexibility in building your game objects.

In your project, the nodes you add are organized into a *tree* structure. In a tree, nodes are added as *children* of other nodes. A particular node can have any number of children, but only one *parent* node. When a group of nodes are collected into a tree, it is called a **scene**, and the tree is referred to as the **scene tree**:

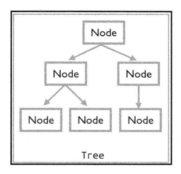

Scenes in Godot are typically used to create and organize the various game objects in your project. You might have a player scene that contains all the nodes and scripts that make the player's character work. Then, you might create another scene that defines the game's map: the obstacles and items that the player must navigate through. You can then combine these various scenes into the final game using *instancing*, which you'll learn about later.

While nodes come with a variety of properties and functions, any node's behavior and capabilities can also be extended by attaching a *script* to the node. This allows you to write code that makes the node do more than it can in its default state. For example, you can add a Sprite node to your scene to display an image, but if you want that image to move or disappear when clicked, you'll need to add a script to create that behavior.

Scripting in Godot

At the time of writing, Godot provides three official languages for scripting nodes: GDScript, VisualScript, and C#. GDScript is the dedicated built-in language, providing the tightest integration with the engine, and is the most straightforward to use. VisualScript is still very new and in the *testing* stage, and should be avoided until you have a good understanding of Godot's workings. For most projects, C# is best reserved for those portions of the game where there is a specific performance need; most Godot projects will not need this level of additional performance. For those that do, Godot gives the flexibility to use a combination of GDScript and C# where you need them.

In addition to the three supported scripting languages, Godot itself is written in C++ and you can get even more performance and control by extending the engine's functionality directly. See Chapter 7, *Additional Topics*, for information on using other languages and extending the engine.

All of the games in this book use GDScript. For the majority of projects, GDScript is the best choice of language. It is very tightly integrated with Godot's **Application Programming Interface** (**API**), and is designed for rapid development.

About GDScript

GDScript's syntax is very closely modeled on the Python language. If you are familiar with Python already, you will find GDScript very familiar. If you are comfortable with another dynamic language, such as JavaScript, you should find it relatively easy to learn. Python is very often recommended as a good beginner language, and GDScript shares that user-friendliness.

This book assumes you have at least *some* programming experience already. If you've never coded before, you may find it a little more difficult. Learning a game engine is a large task on its own; learning to code at the same time means you've taken on a major challenge. If you find yourself struggling with the code in this book, you may find that working through an introductory Python lesson will help you grasp the basics.

Like Python, GDScript is a *dynamically typed* language, meaning you do not need to declare a variable's type when creating it, and it uses *whitespace* (indentation) to denote code blocks. Overall, the result of using GDScript for your game's logic is that you write less code, which means faster development and fewer mistakes to fix.

To give you an idea of what GDScript looks like, here is a small script that causes a sprite to move from left to right across the screen at a given speed:

```
extends Sprite

var speed = 200

func _ready():
    position = Vector2(100, 100)

func _process(delta):
    position.x += speed * delta
    if position.x > 500:
        position.x = 0
```

Don't worry if this doesn't make sense to you yet. In the following chapters, you'll be writing lots of code, which will be accompanied by explanations of how it all works.

Summary

In this chapter, you were introduced to the concept of a game engine in general and to Godot in particular. Most importantly, you downloaded Godot and launched it!

You learned some important vocabulary that will be used throughout this book when referring to various parts of the Godot editor window. You also learned about the concepts of nodes and scenes, which are the fundamental building blocks of Godot.

You also received some advice on how to approach the projects in this book and game development in general. If you ever find yourself getting frustrated as you are working through this book, go back and reread the *General advice* section. There's a lot to learn, and it's okay if it doesn't all make sense the first time. You'll make five different games over the course of this book, and each one will help you understand things a little bit more.

You're ready to move on to Chapter 2, *Coin Dash*, where you'll start building your first game in Godot.

2
Coin Dash

This first project will guide you through making your first Godot Engine project. You will learn how the Godot editor works, how to structure a project, and how to build a small 2D game.

 Why 2D? In a nutshell, 3D games are much more complex than 2D ones, while many of the underlying game engine features you'll need to know are the same. You should stick to 2D until you have a good understanding of Godot's game development process. At that point, the jump to 3D will be much easier. You'll get an introduction to 3D in this book's fifth and final project.

Important—don't skip this chapter, even if you aren't a complete newcomer to game development. While you may already understand many of the underlying concepts, this project will introduce a number of fundamental Godot features and design paradigms that you'll need to know going forward. You'll build on these concepts as you develop more complex projects.

The game in this chapter is called **Coin Dash**. Your character must move around the screen, collecting as many coins as possible while racing against the clock. When you're finished, the game will look like this:

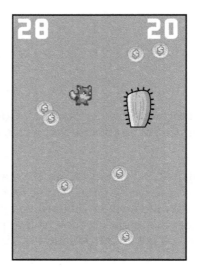

Project setup

Launch Godot and create a new project, making sure to use the `Create Folder` button to ensure that this project's files will be kept separate from other projects. You can download a Zip file of the art and sounds (collectively known as *assets*) for the game here, `https://github.com/PacktPublishing/Godot-Game-Engine-Projects/releases`.

Unzip this file in your new project folder.

In this project, you will make three independent scenes: `Player`, `Coin`, and `HUD`, which will all be combined into the game's `Main` scene. In a larger project, it might be useful to make separate folders to hold each scene's assets and scripts, but for this relatively small game, you can save your scenes and scripts in the root folder, which is referred to as `res://` (**res** is short for **resource**). All resources in your project will be located relative to the `res://` folder. You can see your project folders in the **FileSystem** dock in the upper-left corner:

For example, the images for the coin would be located in `res://assets/coin/`.

This game will use portrait mode, so you need to adjust the size of the game window. Click on the **Project** menu and select **Project Settings**, as shown in the following screenshot:

Look for the **Display/Window** section and set **Width** to 480 and **Height** to 720. Also in this section, set the **Stretch/Mode** to 2D and the **Aspect** to keep. This will ensure that if the user resizes the game window, everything will scale appropriately and not become stretched or deformed. If you like, you can also uncheck the box for **Resizable**, to prevent the window from being resized entirely.

Vectors and 2D coordinate systems

Note: This section is a very brief overview of 2D coordinate systems and does not delve very deeply into vector math. It is intended as a high-level overview of how such topics apply to game development in Godot. Vector math is an essential tool in game development, so if you need a broader understanding of the topic, see Khan Academy's Linear Algebra series (https://www.khanacademy.org/math/linear-algebra).

When working in 2D, you'll be using Cartesian coordinates to identify locations in space. A particular position in 2D space is written as a pair of values, such as (4, 3), representing the position along the x and y axes, respectively. Any position in the 2D plane can be described in this way.

In 2D space, Godot follows the common computer graphics practice of orienting the x axis to the right, and the y axis down:

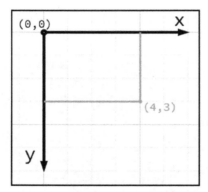

 If you're new to computer graphics or game development, it might seem odd that the positive y axis points downwards instead of upwards, as you likely learned in math class. However, this orientation is very common in computer graphics applications.

Vectors

You can also think of the position (4, 3) as an *offset* from the (0, 0) point, or *origin*. Imagine an arrow pointing from the origin to the point:

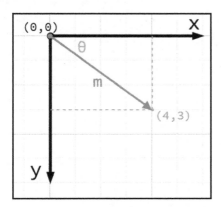

This arrow is a *vector*. It represents a great deal of useful information including the point's location, *(4, 3)*, its length, *m*, and its angle from the *x*-axis, *θ*. Altogether, this is a *position vector*, in other words, it describes a position in space. Vectors can also represent movement, acceleration, or any other quantity that has an *x* and a *y* component.

In Godot, vectors (Vector2 for 2D or Vector3 for 3D) are widely used, and you'll use them in the course of building the projects in this book.

Pixel rendering

Vector coordinates in Godot are *floating point* numbers, not *integers*. This means a Vector2 could have a fractional value, such as (1.5, 1.5). Since objects can't be drawn at half pixels, this can cause visual problems for pixel art games where you want to ensure that all the pixels of the textures are drawn.

To address this, open **Project** | **Project Settings** and find the **Rendering/Quality** section in the sidebar and enable **Use Pixel Snap**, as shown in the following screenshot:

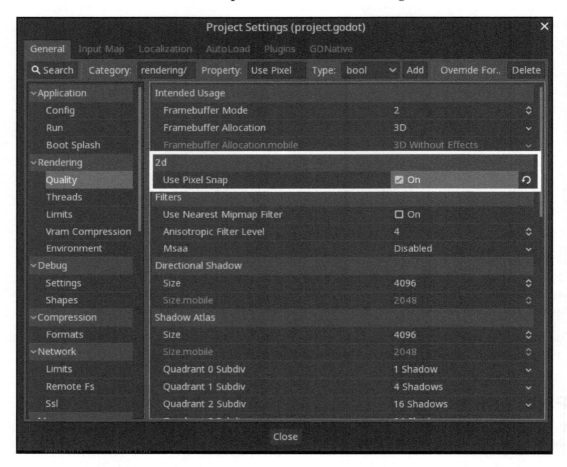

If you're using 2D pixel art in your game, it's a good idea to always enable this setting when you start your project. This setting has no effect in 3D games.

Part 1 – Player scene

The first scene you'll make defines the **Player** object. One of the benefits of creating a separate player scene is that you can test it independently, even before you've created the other parts of the game. This separation of game objects will become more and more helpful as your projects grow in size and complexity. Keeping individual game objects separate from each other makes them easier to troubleshoot, modify, and even replace entirely without affecting other parts of the game. It also makes your player reusable—you can drop the player scene into an entirely different game and it will work just the same.

The player scene will display your character and its animations, respond to user input by moving the character accordingly, and detect collisions with other objects in the game.

Creating the scene

Start by clicking the Add/Create a New Node button and selecting an Area2D. Then, click on its name and change it to Player. Click **Scene | Save Scene** to save the scene. This is the scene's *root* or top-level node. You'll add more functionality to the Player by adding children to this node:

Before adding any children, it's a good idea to make sure you don't accidentally move or resize them by clicking on them. Select the Player node and click the icon next to the lock:

The tooltip will say Make sure the object's children are not selectable, as shown in the preceding screenshot.

 It's a good idea to always do this when creating a new scene. If a body's collision shape or sprite becomes offset or scaled, it can cause unexpected errors and be difficult to fix. With this option, the node and all of its children will always move together.

Sprite animation

With `Area2D`, you can detect when other objects overlap or run into the player, but `Area2D` doesn't have an appearance on its own, so click on the `Player` node and add an `AnimatedSprite` node as a child. The `AnimatedSprite` will handle the appearance and animations for your player. Note that there is a warning symbol next to the node. An `AnimatedSprite` requires a `SpriteFrames` resource, which contains the animation(s) it can display. To create one, find the Frames property in the Inspector and click **<null>** | **New SpriteFrames**:

Next, in the same location, click **<SpriteFrames>** to open the **SpriteFrames** panel:

On the left is a list of animations. Click the **default** one and rename it to `run`. Then, click the **Add** button and create a second animation named `idle` and a third named `hurt`.

In the **FileSystem** dock on the left, find the `run`, `idle`, and `hurt` player images and drag them into the corresponding animations:

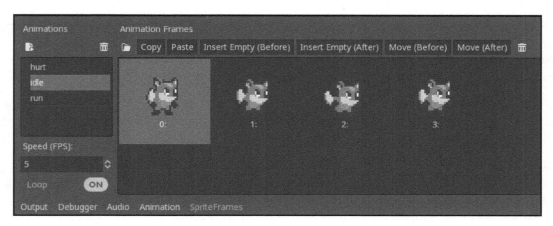

Each animation has a default speed setting of **5** frames per second. This is a little too slow, so click on each of the animations and set the **Speed (FPS)** setting to **8**. In the **Inspector**, check **On** next to the **Playing** property and choose an **Animation** to see the animations in action:

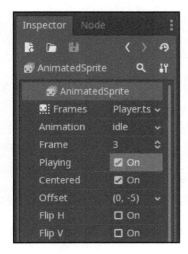

Later, you'll write code to select between these animations, depending on what the player is doing. But first, you need to finish setting up the player's nodes.

Collision shape

When using `Area2D`, or one of the other collision objects in Godot, it needs to have a shape defined, or it can't detect collisions. A collision shape defines the region that the object occupies and is used to detect overlaps and/or collisions. Shapes are defined by `Shape2D`, and include rectangles, circles, polygons, and other types of shapes.

For convenience, when you need to add a shape to an area or physics body, you can add a `CollisionShape2D` as a child. You then select the type of shape you want and you can edit its size in the editor.

Add a `CollisionShape2D` as a child of `Player` (make sure you don't add it as a child of the `AnimatedSprite`). This will allow you to determine the player's *hitbox*, or the bounds of its collision area. In the **Inspector**, next to **Shape**, click **<null>** and choose **New RectangleShape2D**. Adjust the shape's size to cover the sprite:

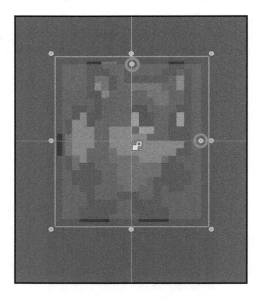

 Be careful not to scale the shape's outline! Only use the size handles (red) to adjust the shape! Collisions will not work properly with a scaled collision shape.

You may have noticed that the collision shape is not centered on the sprite. That is because the sprites themselves are not centered vertically. We can fix this by adding a small offset to the `AnimatedSprite`. Click on the node and look for the **Offset** property in the **Inspector**. Set it to `(0, -5)`.

When you're finished, your `Player` scene should look like this:

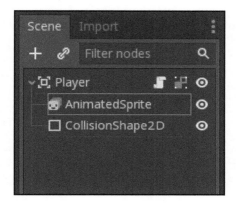

Scripting the Player

Now, you're ready to add a script. Scripts allow you to add additional functionality that isn't provided by the built-in nodes. Click the `Player` node and click the **Add Script** button:

In the **Script Settings** window, you can leave the default settings as they are. If you've remembered to save the scene (see the preceding screenshot), the script will automatically be named to match the scene's name. Click **Create** and you'll be taken to the script window. Your script will contain some default comments and hints. You can remove the comments (lines starting with #). Refer to the following code snippet:

```
extends Area2D

# class member variables go here, for example:
# var a = 2
# var b = "textvar"

func _ready():
 # Called every time the node is added to the scene.
 # Initialization here
 pass

#func _process(delta):
# # Called every frame. Delta is time since last frame.
# # Update game logic here.
# pass
```

The first line of every script will describe what type of node it is attached to. Next, you'll define your class variables:

```
extends Area2D

export (int) var speed
var velocity = Vector2()
var screensize = Vector2(480, 720)
```

Using the `export` keyword on the `speed` variable allows you to set its value in the Inspector, as well as letting the **Inspector** know what type of data the variable should contain. This can be very handy for values that you want to be able to adjust, just like you adjust a node's built-in properties. Click on the `Player` node and set the **Speed** property to **350**, as shown in the following screenshot:

`velocity` will contain the character's current movement speed and direction, and `screensize` will be used to set the limits of the player's movement. Later, the game's main scene will set this variable, but for now you will set it manually so you can test.

Moving the Player

Next, you'll use the `_process()` function to define what the player will do. The `_process()` function is called on every frame, so you'll use it to update elements of your game that you expect to be changing often. You need the player to do three things:

- Check for keyboard input
- Move in the given direction
- Play the appropriate animation

First, you need to check the inputs. For this game, you have four directional inputs to check (the four arrow keys). Input actions are defined in the project settings under the **Input Map** tab. In this tab, you can define custom events and assign different keys, mouse actions, or other inputs to them. By default, Godot has events assigned to the keyboard arrows, so you can use them for this project.

You can detect whether an input is pressed using `Input.is_action_pressed()`, which returns `true` if the key is held down and `false` if it is not. Combining the states of all four buttons will give you the resultant direction of movement. For example, if you hold `right` and `down` at the same time, the resulting velocity vector will be `(1, 1)`. In this case, since we're adding a horizontal and a vertical movement together, the player would move *faster* than if they just moved horizontally.

You can prevent that by *normalizing* the velocity, which means setting its **length** to **1**, then multiplying it by the desired speed:

```
func get_input():
    velocity = Vector2()
    if Input.is_action_pressed("ui_left"):
        velocity.x -= 1
    if Input.is_action_pressed("ui_right"):
        velocity.x += 1
    if Input.is_action_pressed("ui_up"):
        velocity.y -= 1
    if Input.is_action_pressed("ui_down"):
        velocity.y += 1
    if velocity.length() > 0:
        velocity = velocity.normalized() * speed
```

By grouping all of this code together in a `get_input()` function, you make it easier to change things later. For example, you could decide to change to an analog joystick or other type of controller. Call this function from `_process()` and then change the player's `position` by the resulting `velocity`. To prevent the player from leaving the screen, you can use the `clamp()` function to limit the position to a minimum and maximum value:

```
func _process(delta):
    get_input()
    position += velocity * delta
    position.x = clamp(position.x, 0, screensize.x)
    position.y = clamp(position.y, 0, screensize.y)
```

Click Play the Edited Scene (*F6*) and confirm that you can move the player around the screen in all directions.

About delta

The `_process()` function includes a parameter called `delta` that is then multiplied by the velocity. What is `delta`?

The game engine attempts to run at a consistent 60 frames per second. However, this can change due to computer slowdowns, either in Godot or from the computer itself. If the frame rate is not consistent, then it will affect the movement of your game objects. For example, consider an object set to move 10 pixels every frame. If everything is running smoothly, this will translate to moving 600 pixels in one second. However, if some of those frames take longer, then there may only have been 50 frames in that second, so the object only moved 500 pixels.

Godot, like most game engines and frameworks, solves this by passing you `delta`, which is the elapsed time since the previous frame. Most of the time, this will be around 0.016 s (or around 16 milliseconds). If you then take your desired speed (600 px/s) and multiply by delta, you will get a movement of exactly 10. If, however, the `delta` increased to 0.3, then the object will be moved 18 pixels. Overall, the movement speed remains consistent and independent of the frame rate.

As a side benefit, you can express your movement in units of px/s rather than px/frame, which is easier to visualize.

Choosing animations

Now that the player can move, you need to change which animation the AnimatedSprite is playing based on whether it is moving or standing still. The art for the run animation faces to the right, which means it should be flipped horizontally (using the **Flip H** property) for movement to the left. Add this to the end of your _process() function:

```
if velocity.length() > 0:
    $AnimatedSprite.animation = "run"
    $AnimatedSprite.flip_h = velocity.x < 0
else:
    $AnimatedSprite.animation = "idle"
```

Note that this code takes a little shortcut. flip_h is a Boolean property, which means it can be true or false. A Boolean value is also the result of a comparison like <. Because of this, we can set the property equal to the result of the comparison. This one line is equivalent to writing it out like this:

```
if velocity.x < 0:
    $AnimatedSprite.flip_h = true
else:
    $AnimatedSprite.flip_h = false
```

Play the scene again and check that the animations are correct in each case. Make sure **Playing** is set to **On** in the AnimatedSprite so that the animations will play.

Starting and Ending the Player's Movement

When the game starts, the main scene will need to inform the player that the game has begun. Add the start() function as follows, which the main scene will use to set the player's starting animation and position:

```
func start(pos):
    set_process(true)
    position = pos
    $AnimatedSprite.animation = "idle"
```

The die() function will be called when the player hits an obstacle or runs out of time:

```
func die():
    $AnimatedSprite.animation = "hurt"
    set_process(false)
```

Setting `set_process(false)` causes the `_process()` function to no longer be called for this node. That way, when the player has died, they can't still be moved by key input.

Preparing for collisions

The player should detect when it hits a coin or an obstacle, but you haven't made them do so yet. That's OK, because you can use Godot's *signal* functionality to make it work. Signals are a way for nodes to send out messages that other nodes can detect and react to. Many nodes have built-in signals to alert you when a body collides, for example, or when a button is pressed. You can also define custom signals for your own purposes.

Signals are used by *connecting* them to the node(s) that you want to listen and respond to. This connection can be made in the Inspector or in the code. Later in the project, you'll learn how to connect signals in both ways.

Add the following to the top of the script (after `extends Area2D`):

```
signal pickup
signal hurt
```

These define custom signals that your player will *emit* (send out) when they touch a coin or an obstacle. The touches will be detected by the `Area2D` itself. Select the `Player` node and click the **Node** tab next to the **Inspector** to see the list of signals the player can emit:

Note your custom signals are there as well. Since the other objects will also be `Area2D` nodes, you want the `area_entered()` signal. Select it and click **Connect**. Click **Connect** on the **Connecting Signal** window—you don't need to change any of those settings. Godot will automatically create a new function called `_on_Player_area_entered()` in your script.

When connecting a signal, instead of having Godot create a function for you, you can also give the name of an existing function that you want to link the signal to. Toggle the **Make Function** switch to **Off** if you don't want Godot to create the function for you.

Add the following code to this new function:

```
func _on_Player_area_entered( area ):
    if area.is_in_group("coins"):
        area.pickup()
        emit_signal("pickup")
    if area.is_in_group("obstacles"):
        emit_signal("hurt")
        die()
```

When another `Area2D` is detected, it will be passed in to the function (using the `area` variable). The coin object will have a `pickup()` function that defines the coin's behavior when picked up (playing an animation or sound, for example). When you create the coins and obstacles, you'll assign them to the appropriate *group* so they can be detected.

To summarize, here is the complete player script so far:

```
extends Area2D

signal pickup
signal hurt

export (int) var speed
var velocity = Vector2()
var screensize = Vector2(480, 720)

func get_input():
    velocity = Vector2()
    if Input.is_action_pressed("ui_left"):
        velocity.x -= 1
    if Input.is_action_pressed("ui_right"):
        velocity.x += 1
    if Input.is_action_pressed("ui_up"):
        velocity.y -= 1
    if Input.is_action_pressed("ui_down"):
```

```
                velocity.y += 1
        if velocity.length() > 0:
            velocity = velocity.normalized() * speed

    func _process(delta):
        get_input()
        position += velocity * delta
        position.x = clamp(position.x, 0, screensize.x)
        position.y = clamp(position.y, 0, screensize.y)

        if velocity.length() > 0:
            $AnimatedSprite.animation = "run"
            $AnimatedSprite.flip_h = velocity.x < 0
        else:
            $AnimatedSprite.animation = "idle"

    func start(pos):
        set_process(true)
        position = pos
        $AnimatedSprite.animation = "idle"

    func die():
        $AnimatedSprite.animation = "hurt"
        set_process(false)

    func _on_Player_area_entered( area ):
        if area.is_in_group("coins"):
            area.pickup()
            emit_signal("pickup")
        if area.is_in_group("obstacles"):
            emit_signal("hurt")
            die()
```

Part 2 – Coin scene

In this part, you'll make the coins for the player to collect. This will be a separate scene describing all of the properties and behavior of a single coin. Once saved, the main scene will load the coin scene and create multiple *instances* (that is, copies) of it.

Node setup

Click **Scene** | **New Scene** and add the following nodes. Don't forget to set the children to not be selected, like you did with the `Player` scene:

- `Area2D` (named `Coin`)
- `AnimatedSprite`
- `CollisionShape2D`

Make sure to save the scene once you've added the nodes.

Set up the `AnimatedSprite` like you did in the Player scene. This time, you only have one animation: a shine/sparkle effect that makes the coin look less flat and boring. Add all the frames and set the **Speed (FPS)** to `12`. The images are a little too large, so set the **Scale** of `AnimatedSprite` to `(0.5, 0.5)`. In the `CollisionShape2D`, use a `CircleShape2D` and size it to cover the coin image. Don't forget: never use the scale handles when sizing a collision shape. The circle shape has a single handle that adjusts the circle's radius.

Using groups

Groups provide a tagging system for nodes, allowing you to identify similar nodes. A node can belong to any number of groups. You need to ensure that all coins will be in a group called `coins` for the player script to react correctly to touching the coin. Select the `Coin` node and click the **Node** tab (the same tab where you found the signals) and choose **Groups**. Type `coins` in the box and click **Add**, as shown in the following screenshot:

Script

Next, add a script to the `Coin` node. If you choose **Empty** in the **Template** setting, Godot will create an empty script without any comments or suggestions. The code for the coin's script is much shorter than the code for the player's:

```
extends Area2D

func pickup():
    queue_free()
```

The `pickup()` function is called by the player script and tells the coin what to do when it's been collected. `queue_free()` is Godot's node removal method. It safely removes the node from the tree and deletes it from memory along with all of its children. Later, you'll add a visual effect here, but for now the coin disappearing is good enough.

> `queue_free()` doesn't delete the object immediately, but rather adds it to a queue to be deleted at the end of the current frame. This is safer than immediately deleting the node, because other code running in the game may still need the node to exist. By waiting until the end of the frame, Godot can be sure that all code that may access the node has completed and the node can be removed safely.

Part 3 – Main scene

The `Main` scene is what ties all the pieces of the game together. It will manage the player, the coins, the timer, and the other pieces of the game.

Node setup

Create a new scene and add a node named `Main`. To add the player to the scene, click the Instance button and select your saved `Player.tscn`:

Now, add the following nodes as children of Main, naming them as follows:

- TextureRect (named Background)—for the background image
- Node (named CoinContainer)—to hold all the coins
- Position2D (named PlayerStart)—to mark the starting position of the Player
- Timer (named GameTimer)—to track the time limit

Make sure Background is the first child node. Nodes are drawn in the order shown, so the background will be *behind* the player in this case. Add an image to the Background node by dragging the grass.png image from the assets folder into the **Texture** property. Change the **Stretch Mode** to **Tile** and then click **Layout** | **Full Rect** to size the frame to the size of the screen, as shown in the following screenshot:

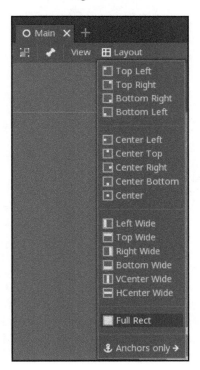

Set the **Position** of the PlayerStart node to (240, 350).

Your scene layout should look like this:

Main script

Add a script to the Main node (use the Empty template) and add the following variables:

```
extends Node

export (PackedScene) var Coin
export (int) var playtime

var level
var score
var time_left
var screensize
var playing = false
```

The Coin and Playtime properties will now appear in the Inspector when you click on
Main. Drag Coin.tscn from the **FileSystem** panel and drop it in the Coin property.
Set Playtime to 30 (this is the amount of time the game will last). The remaining variables
will be used later in the code.

Initializing

Next, add the _ready() function:

```
func _ready():
    randomize()
    screensize = get_viewport().get_visible_rect().size
    $Player.screensize = screensize
    $Player.hide()
```

In GDScript, you can use $ to refer to a particular node by name. This allows you to find the size of the screen and assign it to the player's screensize variable. hide() makes the player start out invisible (you'll make them appear when the game actually starts).

In the $ notation, the node name is relative to the node running the script. For example, $Node1/Node2 would refer to a node (Node2) that is the child of Node1, which itself is a child of the currently running script. Godot's autocomplete will suggest node names from the tree as you type. Note that if the node's name contains spaces, you must put quote marks around it, for example, $"My Node".

 You must use randomize() if you want your sequence of "random" numbers to be different every time you run the scene. Technically speaking, this selects a random *seed* for the random number generator.

Starting a new game

Next, the new_game() function will initialize everything for a new game:

```
func new_game():
    playing = true
    level = 1
    score = 0
    time_left = playtime
    $Player.start($PlayerStart.position)
    $Player.show()
    $GameTimer.start()
    spawn_coins()
```

In addition to setting the variables to their starting values, this function calls the Player's start() function to ensure it moves to the proper starting location. The game timer is started, which will count down the remaining time in the game.

You also need a function that will create a number of coins based on the current level:

```
func spawn_coins():
    for i in range(4 + level):
        var c = Coin.instance()
        $CoinContainer.add_child(c)
        c.screensize = screensize
        c.position = Vector2(rand_range(0, screensize.x),
        rand_range(0, screensize.y))
```

In this function, you create a number of *instances* of the Coin object (in code this time, rather than by clicking the **Instance a Scene** button), and add it as a child of the CoinContainer. Whenever you instance a new node, it must be added to the tree using add_child(). Finally, you pick a random location for the coin to appear in. You'll call this function at the start of every level, generating more coins each time.

Eventually, you'll want new_game() to be called when the player clicks the start button. For now, to test if everything is working, add new_game() to the end of your _ready() function and click Play the Project (*F5*). When you are prompted to choose a main scene, choose Main.tscn. Now, whenever you play the project, the Main scene will be started.

At this point, you should see your player and five coins appear on the screen. When the player touches a coin, it disappears.

Checking for remaining coins

The main script needs to detect whether the player has picked up all of the coins. Since the coins are all children of CoinCointainer, you can use get_child_count() on this node to find out how many coins remain. Put this in the _process() function so that it will be checked every frame:

```
func _process(delta):
    if playing and $CoinContainer.get_child_count() == 0:
        level += 1
        time_left += 5
        spawn_coins()
```

If no more coins remain, then the player advances to the next level.

Part 4 – User Interface

The final piece your game needs is a **user interface** (**UI**). This is an interface to display information that the player needs to see during gameplay. In games, this is also referred to as a **Heads-Up Display** (**HUD**), because the information appears as an overlay on top of the game view. You'll also use this scene to display a start button.

The HUD will display the following information:

- Score
- Time remaining
- A message, such as Game Over
- A start button

Node setup

Create a new scene and add a `CanvasLayer` node named `HUD`. A `CanvasLayer` node allows you to draw your UI elements on a layer above the rest of the game, so that the information it displays doesn't get covered up by any game elements like the player or the coins.

Godot provides a wide variety of UI elements that may be used to create anything from indicators such as health bars to complex interfaces such as inventories. In fact, the Godot editor that you are using to make this game is built in Godot using these elements. The basic nodes for UI elements are extended from `Control`, and appear with green icons in the node list. To create your UI, you'll use various `Control` nodes to position, format, and display information. Here is what the `HUD` will look like when complete:

Anchors and margins

Control nodes have a position and size, but they also have properties called **anchors** and **margins**. Anchors define the origin, or the reference point, for the edges of the node, relative to the parent container. Margins represent the distance from the control node's edge to its corresponding anchor. Margins update automatically when you move or resize a control node.

Message label

Add a `Label` node to the scene and change its name to `MessageLabel`. This label will display the game's title, as well as **Game Over** when the game ends. This label should be centered on the game screen. You could drag it with the mouse, but to place UI elements precisely, you should use the Anchor properties.

Select **View** | **Show Helpers** to display pins that will help you see the anchor positions, then click on the **Layout** menu and select **HCenter Wide**:

The `MessageLabel` now spans the width of the screen and is centered vertically. The **Text** property in the **Inspector** sets what text the label displays. Set it to **Coin Dash**! and set **Align** and **Valign** to **Center**.

The default font for `Label` nodes is very small, so the next step is to assign a custom font. Scroll down to the **Custom Fonts** section in the **Inspector** and select **New DynamicFont**, as shown in the following screenshot:

Now, click on **DynamicFont** and you can adjust the font settings. From the **FileSystem** dock, drag the `Kenney Bold.ttf` font and drop it in the **Font Data** property. Set **Size** to 48, as shown in the following screenshot:

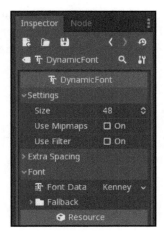

Score and time display

The top of the HUD will display the player's score and the time remaining on the clock. Both of these will be Label nodes, arranged at opposite sides of the game screen. Rather than position them separately, you'll use a Container node to manage their positions.

Containers

UI containers automatically arrange the positions of their child Control nodes (including other Containers). You can use them to add padding around elements, center them, or arrange elements in rows or columns. Each type of Container has special properties that control how they arrange their children. You can see these properties in the **Custom Constants** section of the **Inspector**.

 Remember that containers *automatically* arrange their children. If you move or resize a **Control** that's inside a Container node, you'll find it snaps back to its original position. You can manually arrange controls *or* arrange them with a container, but not both.

To manage the score and time labels, add a MarginContainer node to the HUD. Use the **Layout** menu to set the anchors to **Top Wide**. In the **Custom Constants** section, set **Margin Right**, **Margin Top**, and **Margin Left** to 10. This will add some padding so that the text isn't against the edge of the screen.

Since the score and time labels will use the same font settings as the MessageLabel, it will save time if you duplicate it. Click on MessageLabel and press *Ctrl + D* (*Cmd + D* on macOS) twice to create two duplicate labels. Drag them both and drop them on the MarginContainer to make them its children. Name one ScoreLabel and the other TimeLabel and set the **Text** property to 0 for both. Set **Align** to **Left** for ScoreLabel and **Right** for TimeLabel.

Updating UI via GDScript

Add a script to the HUD node. This script will update the UI elements when their properties need to change, updating the score text whenever a coin is collected, for example. Refer to the following code:

```
extends CanvasLayer

signal start_game
```

```
func update_score(value):
    $MarginContainer/ScoreLabel.text = str(value)

func update_timer(value):
    $MarginContainer/TimeLabel.txt = str(value)
```

The `Main` scene's script will call these functions to update the display whenever there is a change in value. For the `MessageLabel`, you also need a timer to make it disappear after a brief period. Add a `Timer` node and change its name to `MessageTimer`. In the **Inspector**, set its **Wait Time** to 2 seconds and check the box to set **One Shot** to **On**. This ensures that, when started, the timer will only run once, rather than repeating. Add the following code:

```
func show_message(text):
    $MessageLabel.text = text
    $MessageLabel.show()
    $MessageTimer.start()
```

In this function, you display the message and start the timer. To hide the message, connect the `timeout()` signal of `MessageTimer` and add this:

```
func _on_MessageTimer_timeout():
    $MessageLabel.hide()
```

Using buttons

Add a `Button` node and change its name to `StartButton`. This button will be displayed before the game starts, and when clicked, it will hide itself and send a signal to the `Main` scene to start the game. Set the **Text** property to **Start** and change the custom font like you did with the `MessageLabel`. In the **Layout** menu, choose **Center Bottom**. This will put the button at the very bottom of the screen, so move it up a little bit either by pressing the *Up* arrow key or by editing the margins and setting **Top** to −150 and **Bottom** to −50.

When a button is clicked, a signal is sent out. In the **Node** tab for the `StartButton`, connect the `pressed()` signal:

```
func _on_StartButton_pressed():
    $StartButton.hide()
    $MessageLabel.hide()
    emit_signal("start_game")
```

The HUD emits the `start_game` signal to notify `Main` that it's time to start a new game.

Game over

The final task for your UI is to react to the game ending:

```
func show_game_over():
    show_message("Game Over")
    yield($MessageTimer, "timeout")
    $StartButton.show()
    $MessageLabel.text = "Coin Dash!"
    $MessageLabel.show()
```

In this function, you need the Game Over message to be displayed for two seconds and then disappear, which is what `show_message()` does. However, you also want to show the start button once the message has disappeared. The `yield()` function pauses execution of the function until the given node (`MessageTimer`) emits a given signal (`timeout`). Once the signal is received, the function continues, returning you to the initial state so that you can play again.

Adding the HUD to Main

Now, you need to set up the communication between the Main scene and the HUD. Add an instance of the HUD scene to the Main scene. In the Main scene, connect the `timeout()` signal of `GameTimer` and add the following:

```
func _on_GameTimer_timeout():
    time_left -= 1
    $HUD.update_timer(time_left)
    if time_left <= 0:
        game_over()
```

Every time the `GameTimer` times out (every second), the remaining time is reduced. Next, connect the `pickup()` and `hurt()` signals of the `Player`:

```
func _on_Player_pickup():
    score += 1
    $HUD.update_score(score)

func _on_Player_hurt():
    game_over()
```

Several things need to happen when the game ends, so add the following function:

```
func game_over():
    playing = false
    $GameTimer.stop()
    for coin in $CoinContainer.get_children():
        coin.queue_free()
    $HUD.show_game_over()
    $Player.die()
```

This function halts the game, and also loops through the coins and removes any that are remaining, as well as calling the HUD's show_game_over() function.

Finally, the StartButton needs to activate the new_game() function. Click on the HUD instance and select its new_game() signal. In the signal connection dialog, click **Make Function** to **Off** and in the **Method In Node** field, type new_game. This will connect the signal to the existing function rather than creating a new one. Take a look at the following screenshot:

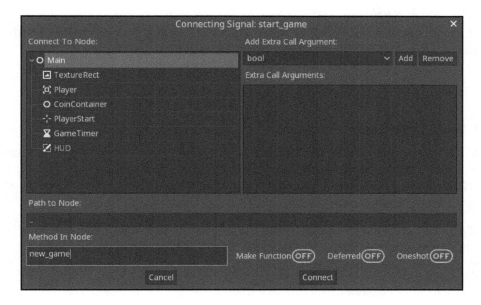

Remove new_game() from the _ready() function and add these two lines to the new_game() function:

```
$HUD.update_score(score)
$HUD.update_timer(time_left)
```

Now, you can play the game! Confirm that all the parts are working as intended: the score, the countdown, the game ending and restarting, and so on. If you find a piece that's not working, go back and check the step where you created it, as well as the step(s) where it was connected to the rest of the game.

Part 5 – Finishing up

You have created a working game, but it still could be made to feel a little more exciting. Game developers use the term *juice* to describe the things that make the game feel good to play. Juice can include things like sound, visual effects, or any other addition that adds to the player's enjoyment, without necessarily changing the nature of the gameplay.

In this section, you'll add some small *juicy* features to finish up the game.

Visual effects

When you pick up the coins, they just disappear, which is not very appealing. Adding a visual effect will make it much more satisfying to collect lots of coins.

Start by adding a Tween node to the Coin scene.

What is a tween?

A **tween** is a way to interpolate (change gradually) some value over time (from a start value to an end value) using a particular function. For example, you might choose a function that steadily changes the value or one that starts slow but ramps up in speed. Tweening is also sometimes referred to as *easing*.

When using a Tween node in Godot, you can assign it to alter one or more properties of a node. In this case, you're going to increase the Scale of the coin and also cause it to fade out using the Modulate property.

Add this line to the _ready() function of Coin:

```
$Tween.interpolate_property($AnimatedSprite, 'scale',
                            $AnimatedSprite.scale,
                            $AnimatedSprite.scale * 3, 0.3,
                            Tween.TRANS_QUAD,
                            Tween.EASE_IN_OUT)
```

The `interpolate_property()` function causes the `Tween` to change a node's property. There are seven parameters:

- The node to affect
- The property to alter
- The property's starting value
- The property's ending value
- The duration (in seconds)
- The function to use
- The direction

The tween should start playing when the player picks up the coin. Replace `queue_free()` in the `pickup()` function:

```
func pickup():
    monitoring = false
    $Tween.start()
```

Setting `monitoring` to `false` ensures that the `area_enter()` signal won't be emitted if the player touches the coin during the tween animation.

Finally, the coin should be deleted when the animation finishes, so connect the `Tween` node's `tween_completed()` signal:

```
func _on_Tween_tween_completed(object, key):
    queue_free()
```

Now, when you run the game, you should see the coins growing larger when they're picked up. This is good, but tweens are even more effective when applied to multiple properties at once. You can add another `interpolate_property()`, this time to change the sprite's opacity. This is done by altering the `modulate` property, which is a `Color` object, and changing its alpha channel from 1 (opaque) to 0 (transparent). Refer to the following code:

```
$Tween.interpolate_property($AnimatedSprite, 'modulate',
                    Color(1, 1, 1, 1),
                    Color(1, 1, 1, 0), 0.3,
                    Tween.TRANS_QUAD,
                    Tween.EASE_IN_OUT)
```

Sound

Sound is one of the most important but often neglected pieces of game design. Good sound design can add a huge amount of juice to your game for a very small amount of effort. Sounds can give the player feedback, connect them emotionally to the characters, or even be a part of the gameplay.

For this game, you're going to add three sound effects. In the `Main` scene, add three `AudioStreamPlayer` nodes and name them `CoinSound`, `LevelSound`, and `EndSound`. Drag each sound from the `audio` folder (you can find it under `assets` in the **FileSystem** dock) into the corresponding **Stream** property of each node.

To play a sound, you call the `play()` function on it. Add `$CoinSound.play()` to the `_on_Player_pickup()` function, `$EndSound.play()` to the `game_over()` function, and `$LevelSound.play()` to the `spawn_coins()` function.

Powerups

There are many possibilities for objects that give the player a small advantage or powerup. In this section, you'll add a powerup item that gives the player a small time bonus when collected. It will appear occasionally for a short time, then disappear.

The new scene will be very similar to the `Coin` scene you already created, so click on your `Coin` scene and choose **Scene | Save Scene As** and save it as `Powerup.tscn`. Change the name of the root node to **Powerup** and remove the script by clicking the clear script

button: ▉. You should also disconnect the `area_entered` signal (you'll reconnect it later). In the **Groups** tab, remove the **coins** group by clicking the delete button (it looks like a trash can) and adding it to a new group called `powerups` instead.

In the `AnimatedSprite`, change the images from the coin to the powerup, which you can find in the `res://assets/pow/` folder.

Click to add a new script and copy the code from the `Coin.gd` script. Change the name of `_on_Coin_area_entered` to `_on_Powerup_area_entered` and connect the `area_entered` signal to it again. Remember, this function name will automatically be chosen by the **signal connect** window.

Next, add a `Timer` node named `Lifetime`. This will limit the amount of time the object remains on the screen. Set its **Wait Time** to 2 and both **One Shot** and **Autostart** to `On`. Connect its timeout signal so that it can be removed at the end of the time period:

```
func _on_Lifetime_timeout():
    queue_free()
```

Now, go to your Main scene and add another `Timer` node called `PowerupTimer`. Set its **One Shot** property to **On**. There is also a `Powerup.wav` sound in the `audio` folder you can add with another `AudioStreamPlayer`.

Connect the `timeout` signal and add the following code to spawn a `Powerup`:

```
func _on_PowerupTimer_timeout():
    var p = Powerup.instance()
    add_child(p)
    p.screensize = screensize
    p.position = Vector2(rand_range(0, screensize.x),
                        rand_range(0, screensize.y))
```

The `Powerup` scene needs to be linked by adding a variable, then dragging the scene into the property in the **Inspector**, as you did earlier with the `Coin` scene:

```
export (PackedScene) var Powerup
```

The powerups should appear unpredictably, so the wait time of the `PowerupTimer` needs to be set whenever you begin a new level. Add this to the `_process()` function after the new coins are spawned with `spawn_coins()`:

```
$PowerupTimer.wait_time = rand_range(5, 10)
$PowerupTimer.start()
```

Now that you will have powerups appearing, the last step is to give the player some bonus time when one is collected. Currently, the player script assumes anything it runs into is either a coin or an obstacle. Change the code in `Player.gd` to check for what kind of object has been hit:

```
func _on_Player_area_entered( area ):
    if area.is_in_group("coins"):
        area.pickup()
        emit_signal("pickup", "coin")
    if area.is_in_group("powerups"):
        area.pickup()
        emit_signal("pickup", "powerup")
    if area.is_in_group("obstacles"):
        emit_signal("hurt")
        die()
```

Note that now you're emitting the pickup signal with an additional argument naming the type of object. The corresponding function in `Main.gd` can now be changed to accept that argument and use the `match` statement to decide what action to take:

```
func _on_Player_pickup(type):
    match type:
        "coin":
            score += 1
            $CoinSound.play()
            $HUD.update_score(score)
        "powerup":
            time_left += 5
            $PowerupSound.play()
            $HUD.update_timer(time_left)
```

The `match` statement is a useful alternative to `if` statements, especially when you have a large number of possible values to test.

Try running the game and collecting the powerup. Make sure the sound plays and the timer increases by five seconds.

Coin animation

When you created the `Coin` scene, you added an `AnimatedSprite`, but it isn't playing yet. The coin animation displays a *shimmer* effect traveling across the face of the coin. If all the coins display this at the same time, it will look too regular, so each coin needs a small random delay in its animation.

First, click on the `AnimatedSprite` and then on the *Frames* resource. Make sure **Loop** is set to **Off** and that **Speed** is set to `12`.

Add a `Timer` node to the `Coin` scene, and add this code to _ready():

```
$Timer.wait_time = rand_range(3, 8)
$Timer.start()
```

Now, connect the `timeout()` signal from the `Timer` and add this:

```
func _on_Timer_timeout():
    $AnimatedSprite.frame = 0
    $AnimatedSprite.play()
```

Try running the game and watching for the coins to animate. It's a nice visual effect for a very small amount of effort. You'll notice a lot of effects like this in professional games. Though very subtle, the visual appeal makes for a much more pleasing experience.

The preceding `Powerup` object has a similar animation that you can add in the same manner.

Obstacles

Finally, the game can be made a bit more challenging by introducing an obstacle that the player must avoid. Touching the obstacle will end the game.

Create a new scene for the cactus and add the following nodes:

- `Area2D` (named `Cactus`)
- `Sprite`
- `CollisionShape2D`

Drag the cactus texture from the **FileSystem** dock to the **Texture** property of the `Sprite`. Add a `RectangleShape2D` to the collision shape and size it so that it covers the image. Remember when you added `if area.is_in_group("obstacles")` to the player script? Add the `Cactus` body to the `obstacles` group using the **Node** tab (next to **Inspector**).

Now, add a `Cactus` instance to the `Main` scene and move it to a location in the upper half of the screen (away from where the player spawns). Play the game and see what happens when you run into the cactus.

You may have spotted a problem: coins can spawn behind the cactus, making them impossible to pick up. When the coin is placed, it needs to move if it detects that it's overlapping the obstacle. Connect the coin's `area_entered()` signal and add the following:

```
func _on_Coin_area_entered( area ):
    if area.is_in_group("obstacles"):
        position = Vector2(rand_range(0, screensize.x), rand_range(0,
screensize.y))
```

If you've added the preceding `Powerup` object, you'll need to do the same for its `area_entered` signal.

Summary

In this chapter, you learned the basics of Godot Engine by creating a basic 2D game. You set up the project and created multiple scenes, worked with sprites and animations, captured user input, used *signals* to communicate with events, and created a UI using **Control** nodes. The things you learned here are important skills that you'll use in any Godot project.

Before moving on to the next chapter, look through the project. Do you understand what each node is doing? Are there any bits of code that you don't understand? If so, go back and review that section of the chapter.

Also, feel free to experiment with the game and change things around. One of the best ways to get a good feel for what different parts of the game are doing is to change them and see what happens.

In the next chapter, you'll explore more of Godot's features and learn how to use more node types by building a more complex game.

3

Escape the Maze

In the previous chapter, you learned how Godot's node system works, allowing you to build a complex scene out of smaller building blocks, each providing different functionalities for your game's objects. This process will continue as you move up to larger and more complex projects. However, sometimes you'll find yourself duplicating the same nodes and/or code in more than one different object, and this project will introduce some techniques for reducing the amount of repeated code.

In this chapter, you'll build a game called **Escape the Maze**. In this game, you will be trying to navigate a maze to find the exit while avoiding the roaming enemies:

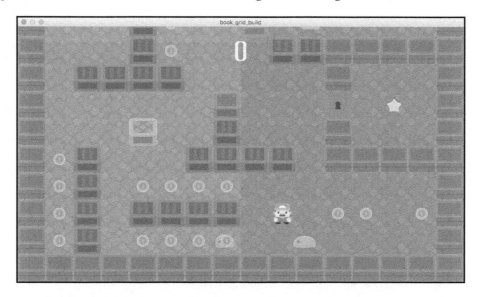

You will learn about the following key topics in this project:

- Inheritance
- Grid-based movement

- Spritesheet animation
- Using TileMaps for level design
- Transitioning between scenes

Project setup

Create a new project and download the project assets from `https://github.com/` `PacktPublishing/Godot-Game-Engine-Projects/releases`.

As you've seen previously, Godot, by default, includes a number of input actions mapped to various keyboard inputs. For example, you used `ui_left` and `ui_right` for arrow key movement in the first project. Often, however, you need a different input from the defaults provided, or you'd like to customize the actions' names. You might also wish to add actions for mouse or gamepad inputs. You can do this in the **Project Settings** window.

Click on the **Input Map** tab and add four new input actions (**left**, **right**, **up**, and **down**) by typing the names into the **Action:** box and clicking **Add**. Then, for each new action, click the + button to add a **Key** action and choose the corresponding arrow key. You can also add WASD controls, if you wish:

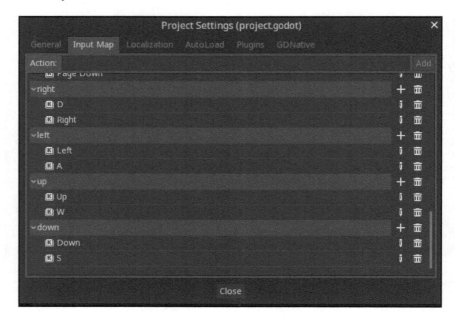

This game will have a variety of objects on the screen. Some of them should detect collisions (the player against the walls, for example), while others should ignore one another (like the enemies versus coins). You can solve this by setting the objects' physics layer and physics layer mask properties. To make these layers easier to work with, Godot allows you to give the game's physics layers custom names.

Click on the **General** tab and find the **Layer Names/2D Physics** section. Name the first four layers as follows:

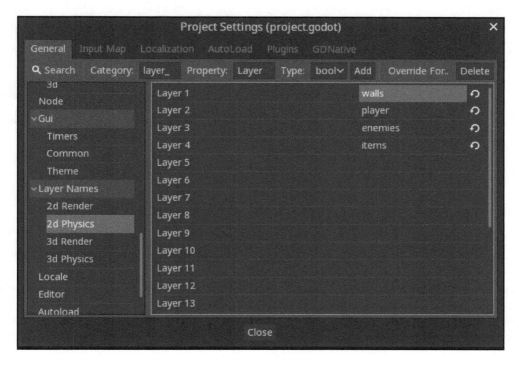

You'll see how the collision layer system works with the various objects in the game later in the project.

Next, in the **Display/Window** section, set the **Mode** to **viewport** and the **Aspect** to **keep**. This will enable you to resize the game window while keeping the display's proportions unchanged. Refer to the following screenshot:

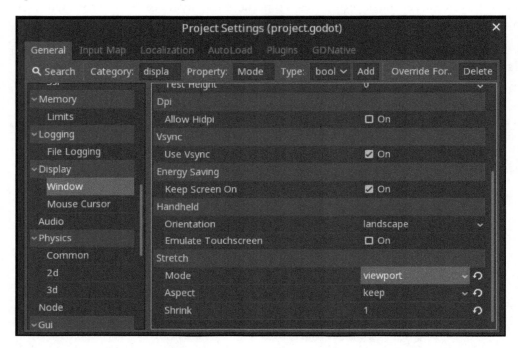

Finally, in the **Rendering/Quality** section, set **Use Pixel Snap** to **On**. This setting is useful, especially for pixel art-styled games, as it ensures that all objects are drawn at whole-number pixel values. Note that this does not affect movement, physics, or other properties; it only applies to the rendering of objects. Refer to the following screenshot:

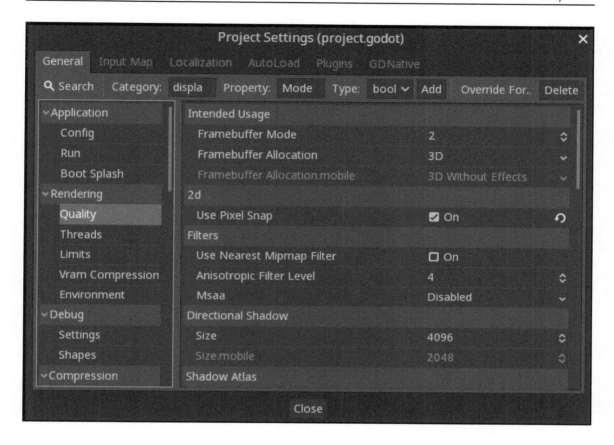

Project organization

As your projects become larger and more involved, you'll find that saving all of your scenes and scripts in the same folder becomes unwieldy.

A common response to this by Godot beginners is to make a `scenes` folder and a `scripts` folder, and to save each type of file in the respective folder. This isn't very effective. Soon, you find yourself hunting through the `scripts` folder, looking for the script you need because it's jumbled up with all the other scripts of your game.

A more logical organization is to create a folder for each type of object. A `player` folder, for example, will hold the player's scene file, script(s), and any other resources that it needs. Organizing your project in this way is much more scalable and can be extended even further if you have a very large number of objects. For example, refer to the following screenshot:

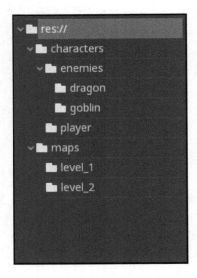

Throughout this project, the examples will assume that each new scene type is being saved in a folder of that type, along with its script. The `Player.tscn` and `Player.gd` files, for example, will be saved in a `player` folder.

Inheritance

In **Object-Oriented Programming** (OOP), inheritance is a powerful tool. Put briefly, you can define a class that *inherits* from another class. An object created using the first class will contain all of the methods and member variables of the master class as well as its own.

Godot is strongly object-oriented, and this gives you the opportunity to use inheritance not just with objects (scripts) but also with scenes, allowing you a great deal of flexibility when designing your game's architecture. It also removes the need to duplicate code—if two objects need to share a set of methods and variables, for example, you can create a common script and let both objects inherit from it. If you make a change to that code, it will apply to both objects.

In this project, the player's character will be controlled by key events, while the mobs will wander around the maze randomly. However, both types of character need to have a number of properties and functions in common:

- A spritesheet containing the four directional movement animations
- An `AnimationPlayer` to play the movement animations
- Grid-based movement (the character can only move one full *tile* at a time)
- Collision detection (the character can't move through walls)

By using inheritance, you can create a generic `Character` scene containing the nodes that all characters need. The player and mob scenes can inherit the shared nodes from that scene. Similarly, the actual movement code (though not the controls) will be identical between player and mob, so they can both inherit from the same script to handle movement.

Character scene

Start creating the `Character` scene by adding an `Area2D` and naming it `Character`. `Area2D` is a good choice for this type of character because its main function will be to detect overlaps—when it moves onto an item or enemy, for example.

Add the following children:

- `Sprite`
- `CollisionShape2D`
- `Tween` (named `MoveTween`)
- `AnimationPlayer`

Leave the `Sprite` without a texture, but in the **Inspector**, under the **Animation** section of the `Sprite`, set its **Vframes** and **Hframes** properties to 4 and 5, respectively. This tells Godot to slice the texture into a 5 x 4 grid of individual images.

The spritesheets you'll use for the player and the enemy are arranged in exactly this pattern, with each row containing the animation frames for a single direction of movement:

When a spritesheet has been sliced using the **Vframes** and **Hframes** properties, you can use the **Frame** property to set which individual frame to use. In the preceding player sheet, the left-facing animation would use frames 5 through 9 (counting from frame 0 in the upper-left corner). You'll use an `AnimationPlayer` to change the **Frame** property below. Refer to the following screenshot:

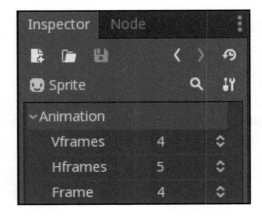

Next, create a new `RectangleShape2D` in the collision shape's Shape. Click on the new **<RectangleShape2D>** and set its **Extents** property in the **Inspector** to (16, 16). Note that **Extents** measures the distance from the center in each direction, so this results in a collision shape that is 32 by 32 pixels.

Because all the characters are drawn to the same scale, we can be confident that the same sized collision shape will work for all characters. If this isn't the case with the art you're using, you can skip setting the collision shape here and configure it later for the individual inherited scenes.

Animations

Create four new animations in the `AnimationPlayer` node. Name them to match the four directions you used in the input actions (**left, right, up,** and **down**). It's important that the spelling matches here: the names of the input actions must have the same spelling and capitalization as the animation names. If you are inconsistent in naming, it will make things much more difficult when you get to the scripting stage. Take a look at the following screenshot:

For each animation, set the **Length** to 1 and the **Step** to 0.2. These properties are located at the bottom of the **Animation** panel:

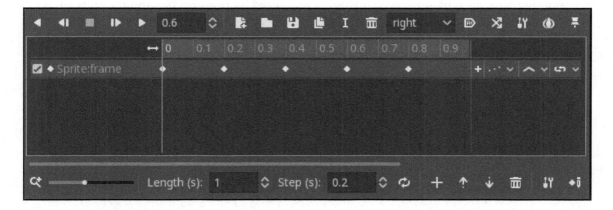

Starting with the **down** animation, click on the `Sprite` node and set its **Frame** property to 0. Click the key icon next to the **Frame** property and confirm that you want to add a new track for the **Frame** property:

The **Frame** property will automatically be incremented by one and the animation track will be advanced by one step (0.2 seconds). Click the key again until you've reached frame 4. You should now have five keyframes on the animation track. If you drag the bar back and forth, you'll see the **Frame** property change as you reach each keyframe:

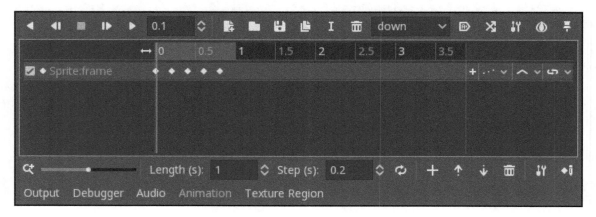

If, for some reason, you find that the frames aren't correct, you can delete any of the keyframes by clicking on the dot and pressing *Delete* on your keyboard, or right-clicking on the dot and choosing **Remove Selection**. Remember, whatever value you set **Frame** to, that will be the value of the keyframe when you press the **Add Keyframe** button. You can also click and drag keyframes to change their order in the timeline.

Repeat the process for the other animations, using the following table to guide you on which keyframes to use for each direction:

Animation	Frames
Down	0, 1, 2, 3, 4
Left	5, 6, 7, 8, 9
Right	10, 11, 12, 13, 14
Up	15, 16, 17, 18, 19

As long as the spritesheet for a character follows the same 5 x 4 arrangement, this `AnimationPlayer` configuration will work, and you won't need to create separate animations for each character. In larger projects, it can be a huge time-saver to create all your spritesheet animations while following a common pattern.

Collision detection

Because the characters are moving on a grid, they need to either move the full distance to the next tile or not at all. This means that, before moving, the character needs to check to see if the move is possible. One way to test if an adjacent square has anything in it is by using a *raycast*. **Raycasting** means extending a ray from the character's position to a given destination. If the ray encounters any object along the way, it will report that contact. By adding four rays to the character, it can *look* at the squares around it to see if they are unoccupied.

Add four `RayCast2D` nodes and set their names and **Cast To** properties as follows:

Name	Cast To
RayCastRight	(64, 0)
RayCastLeft	(-64, 0)
RayCastDown	(0, 64)
RayCastUp	(0, -64)

Make sure to set the **Enabled** property on each one (RayCast2D options are disabled by default). Your final node setup should look like this:

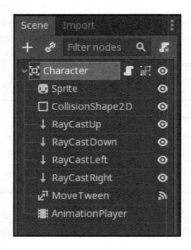

Character script

Now, add a script to the Character node (make sure you've saved the scene first, and the script will automatically be named Character.gd). First, define the class variables:

```
extends Area2D

export (int) var speed

var tile_size = 64
var can_move = true
var facing = 'right'
var moves = {'right': Vector2(1, 0),
             'left': Vector2(-1, 0),
             'up': Vector2(0, -1),
             'down': Vector2(0, 1)}
onready var raycasts = {'right': $RayCastRight,
                        'left': $RayCastLeft,
                        'up': $RayCastUp,
                        'down': $RayCastDown}
```

speed will control the movement and animation speed of the character, allowing you to customize the movement speed. As you learned in Chapter 1, *Introduction*, using export allows you to set the value of a variable via the Inspector. Save the script and set the **Speed** property to 3 in the Inspector.

can_move is a flag that will track whether the character is allowed to move during the current frame. It will be set to false while the movement is underway, preventing a second movement from being started before the previous one has finished. facing is a string denoting the current direction of movement (again, spelled and capitalized exactly like the input actions you created at the beginning of the project). The moves dictionary contains vectors describing the four directions, while the raycasts dictionary contains references to the four raycast nodes. Note that both dictionaries' keys match the input action names.

> When referencing another node during variable declaration, you must use onready to ensure that the variable isn't set before the referenced node is ready. You can think of it as a shortcut to writing the code in the _ready() function. This line:
> onready var sprite = $Sprite
> Is equivalent to writing this:
> var sprite
> func _ready():
>   sprite = $Sprite

The following is the code that will execute a movement from one square to another:

```
func move(dir):
    $AnimationPlayer.playback_speed = speed
    facing = dir
    if raycasts[facing].is_colliding():
        return
    can_move = false
    $AnimationPlayer.play(facing)
    $MoveTween.interpolate_property(self, "position", position,
            position + moves[facing] * tile_size,
            1.0 / speed, Tween.TRANS_SINE, Tween.EASE_IN_OUT)
    $MoveTween.start()
    return true
```

move() takes a direction as an argument. If the RayCast2D for the given direction detects a collision, the move is canceled and the function returns without executing further (note that the return value will be null). Otherwise, it changes facing to the new direction, disables additional movement with can_move, and starts playing the matching animation. To actually perform the movement, the Tween node interpolates the position property from its current value to its current value plus a tile-sized movement in the given direction. The duration (1.0 / speed seconds) is set to match the length of the animation.

Using the Tween.TRANS_SINE transition type results in a pleasing, smooth movement that accelerates up and then down to the final position. Feel free to try other transition types here to alter the movement style.

Finally, to enable movement again, you need to reset can_move when the movement has finished. Connect the tween_completed signal from MoveTween and add the following:

```
func _on_MoveTween_tween_completed( object, key ):
    can_move = true
```

Player scene

The player scene needs to contain all the same nodes we gave to Character. This is where you'll take advantage of the power of inheritance.

Start by making a new scene. However, instead of making a new empty scene, click on **Scene | New Inherited Scene** in the menu. In the **Open Base Scene** window, select res://character/Character.tscn, as shown in the following screenshot:

Rename the root node of this new scene from `Character` to `Player` and save the new scene. Note that all the `Character` nodes are also present. If you make a change to `Character.tscn` and save it, the changes will also take effect in the `Player` scene.

Now, you need to set the Player's physics layers, so find the **Collision** section in the **Inspector** and set the **Layer** and **Mask** properties. **Layer** should be set to **player** only, while **Mask** should show **walls**, **enemies**, and **items**. Refer to the following screenshot:

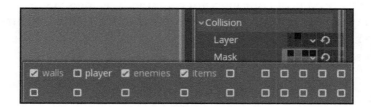

The collision layers system is a powerful tool that allows you to customize which objects can detect each other. The **Layer** property places the object in one or more collision layers, while the **Mask** property defines what layers the object can *see*. If another object is not in one of its mask layers, it will not be detected or collided with.

The only other node that needs to be changed is the `Sprite`, where you need to set the texture. Drag the player spritesheet from the `res://assets` folder and drop it in the **Texture** property of the `Sprite`. Go ahead and test out the animations in the `AnimationPlayer` and make sure they're showing the correct directions. If you find a problem with any of the animations, make sure you fix it in the `Character` scene, and it will automatically be fixed in the `Player` scene as well:

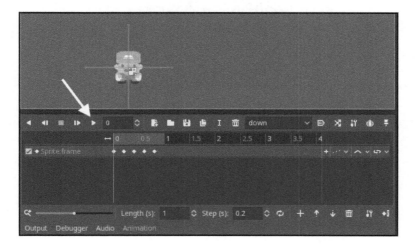

Add a `Camera` node as a child of `Player` and check its **Current** property to **On**. Godot will automatically render whatever the current camera sees in the game window. This will allow you to make maps of any size, and the camera will scroll the map as the player walks around on it. Note that when you add the camera, a purplish box appears, which is centered on the player. This represents the camera's visible region, and because it's a child of the player, it follows the player's movement. If you look at the camera's properties in the **Inspector**, you'll see four **Limit** properties. These are used to stop the camera from scrolling past a certain point; the edge of your map, for example. Try adjusting them and see how the box stops following the `Player` as you drag it around the screen (make sure you're moving the `Player` node itself and not one of its children). Later, the limits will be set automatically by the level itself so that the camera won't scroll "outside" the level.

Player script

The player's script also needs to extend the character's. Remove the attached script (`Character.gd`) by selecting the `Player` node and clicking the **Clear script** button:

Now, click the button again to attach a new script. In the **Attach Node Script** dialog, click the folder icon next to the **Inherits** option and select `Character.gd`:

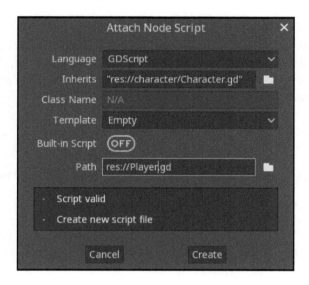

Here is the player script (note that it `extends` the character script):

```
extends "res://character/Character.gd"

signal moved

func _process(delta):
    if can_move:
        for dir in moves.keys():
            if Input.is_action_pressed(dir):
                if move(dir):
                    emit_signal('moved')
```

Because it inherits all the behavior from `Character.gd`, the player will also have the `move()` function. You just need to extend it with code to call `move()` based on the input events. As you've seen before, you can use the `process()` function to check the input state each frame. However, only if `can_move` allows it do you actually check the inputs and call `move()`.

Because you used the names `up`, `down`, `left`, and `right` for the input actions as well as the keys to the `moves` and `raycasts` dictionaries, you can loop through those keys and check each one as an input as well.

Recall that move() returns true if it succeeds. If it does, the player emits the moved signal, which you'll be able to use later with the enemies.

Run the scene and try moving the player character around the screen.

The player doesn't have a level to walk around on yet, but you can go ahead and add the code the player will need later. As the player moves around the level, it will encounter various objects and needs to respond to them. By using signals, you can add the code for this before you've even created the level. Add three more signals to the script:

```
signal dead
signal grabbed_key
signal win
```

Then, connect the area_entered signal of the Player and add this code:

```
func _on_Player_area_entered( area ):
    if area.is_in_group('enemies'):
        emit_signal('dead')
    if area.has_method('pickup'):
        area.pickup()
    if area.type == 'key_red':
        emit_signal('grabbed_key')
    if area.type == 'star':
        emit_signal('win')
```

Whenever the player encounters another Area2D, this function will run. If the object is an enemy, the player loses the game. Note the use of has_method(). This allows you to identify collectible objects by checking whether they have a pickup() method and only call the method if it exists.

Enemy scene

Hopefully, you're seeing how inheritance works by now. You'll create the Enemy scene using the same procedure. Make a new scene inheriting from Character.tscn and name it Enemy. Drag the mob spritesheet, res://assets/slime.png, to the Sprite's **Texture**.

In the **Collision** section of the **Inspector**, set the **Layer** and **Mask** properties. **Layer** should be set to **enemies**, while **Mask** should show **walls** and **player**.

As you did with the `Player`, remove the existing script and attach a new script inheriting from `Character.gd`:

```
extends "res://character/Character.gd"

func _ready():
    can_move = false
    facing = moves.keys()[randi() % 4]
    yield(get_tree().create_timer(0.5), 'timeout')
    can_move = true

func _process(delta):
    if can_move:
        if not move(facing) or randi() % 10 > 5:
            facing = moves.keys()[randi() % 4]
```

The code in the `_ready()` function serves an important purpose: because the enemies are added to the tree *below* the `TileMap` nodes, they'll be processed first. You don't want the enemies to start moving before the walls have been processed, or they could step onto a wall tile and get stuck. You need to have a small delay before they start, which also serves to give the player a moment to prepare. To do this, rather than add a `Timer` node to the scene, you can use the `create_timer()` function of the `SceneTree` to make a one-off timer, yielding execution until its timeout signal fires.

 GDScript's `yield()` function provides a way to *pause* execution of a function until a later time, while allowing the rest of the game to continue running. When passed an object and a named signal, execution will resume when that object emits the given signal.

Every frame, the enemy will move if it is able to. If it runs into a wall (that is, when `move()` returns `null`), or sometimes just randomly, it changes direction. The result will be an unpredictable (and hard to dodge!) enemy movement. Remember that you can adjust the `Player` and `Enemy` speeds independently in their scenes, or change `speed` in the `Character` scene and it will affect them both.

Optional – turn-based movement

For a different style of game, you could put the _process() movement code in a function called _on_Player_moved() instead, and connect it to the player's moved signal. This would make the enemies move only when the player does, giving the game more of a strategic feel, rather than one of fast-paced action.

Creating the level

In this section, you'll create the map where all the action will take place. As the name implies, you'll probably want to make a maze-like level with lots of twists and turns.

Here is a sample level:

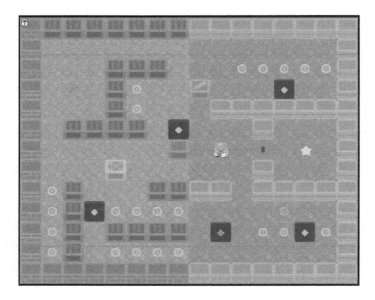

The player's goal is to reach the star. Locked doors can only be opened by picking up the key. The green dots mark the spawn locations of enemies, while the red dot marks the player's start location. The coins are extra items that can be picked up along the way for bonus points. Note that the entire level is larger than the display window. The Camera will scroll the map as the player moves around it.

You'll use the `TileMap` node to create the map. There are several benefits to using a `TileMap` for your level design. First, they make it possible to draw the level's layout by *painting* the tiles onto a grid, which is much faster than placing individual `Sprite` nodes one by one. Secondly, they allow for much larger levels because they are optimized for drawing large numbers of tiles efficiently by batching them together and only drawing the *chunks* of the map that are visible at a given time. Finally, you can add collision shapes to individual tiles and the entire map will act as a single collider, simplifying your collision code.

Once you've completed this section, you'll be able to create as many of these maps as you wish. You can put them in order to give a progression from level to level.

Items

First, create a new scene for the collectable objects that the player can pick up. These items will be spawned by the map when the game is run. Here is the scene tree:

Leave the `Sprite` **Texture** blank. Since you're using this object for multiple items, the texture can be set in the item's script when it's created.

Set the `Pickup` **Collision Layer** to **items** and its **Mask** to **player**. You don't want the enemies collecting the coins before you get there (although that might make for a fun variation on the game where you race to get as many coins as you can before the bad guys gobble them up).

Give the `CollisionShape2D` node a rectangle shape and set its extents to `(32, 32)` (strictly speaking, you can use any shape, as the player will move all the way onto the tile and completely overlap the item anyway).

Here is the script for the `Pickup`:

```
extends Area2D

var textures = {'coin': 'res://assets/coin.png',
                'key_red': 'res://assets/keyRed.png',
                'star': 'res://assets/star.png'}
var type

func _ready():
    $Tween.interpolate_property($Sprite, 'scale', Vector2(1, 1),
        Vector2(3, 3), 0.5, Tween.TRANS_QUAD, Tween.EASE_IN_OUT)
    $Tween.interpolate_property($Sprite, 'modulate',
        Color(1, 1, 1, 1), Color(1, 1, 1, 0), 0.5,
        Tween.TRANS_QUAD, Tween.EASE_IN_OUT)

func init(_type, pos):
    $Sprite.texture = load(textures[_type])
    type = _type
    position = pos

func pickup():
    $CollisionShape2D.disabled = true
    $Tween.start()
```

The `type` variable will be set when the item is created and used to determine what texture the object should use. Using `_type` as the variable name in the function argument lets you use the name without conflicting with `type`, which is already in use.

 Some programming languages use the notion of *private* functions or variables, meaning they are only used locally. The _ naming convention in GDScript is used to visually designate variables or functions that should be regarded as private. Note that they aren't actually any different from any other name; it is merely a visual indication for the programmer.

The pickup effect using `Tween` is similar to the one you used for the coins in Coin Dash—animating the scale and opacity of `Sprite`. Connect the `tween_completed` signal of `Tween` so that the item can be deleted when the effect has finished:

```
func _on_Tween_tween_completed( object, key ):
    queue_free()
```

TileSets

In order to draw a map using a `TileMap`, it must have a `TileSet` assigned to it. The `TileSet` contains all of the individual tile textures, along with any collision shapes they may have.

Depending on how many tiles you have, it can be time-consuming to create a `TileSet`, especially the first time. For that reason, there is a pre-generated `TileSet` included in the `assets` folder titled `tileset.tres`. Feel free to use that instead, but please don't skip the following section. It contains useful information to help you understand how the `TileSet` works.

Creating a TileSet

A `TileSet` in Godot is a type of `Resource`. Examples of other resources include Textures, Animations, and Fonts. They are containers that hold a certain type of data, and are typically saved as `.tres` files.

 By default, Godot saves files in text-based formats, indicated by the `t` in `.tscn` or `.tres`, for example. Text-based files are preferred over binary formats because they are human-readable. They are also more friendly for **Version Control Systems** (**VCS**), which allow you to track file changes over the course of building your project.

To make a `TileSet`, you create a scene with a set of `Sprite` nodes containing the textures from your art assets. You can then add collisions and other properties to those `Sprite` tiles. Once you've created all the tiles, you export the scene as a `TileSet` resource, which can then be loaded by the `TileMap` node.

Here is a screenshot of the `TileSetMaker.tscn` scene, containing the tiles you'll be using to build this game's levels:

Start by adding a `Sprite` node and setting its texture to `res://assets/sokoban_tilesheet.png`. To select a single tile, set the **Region/Enabled** property to **On** and click **Texture Region** at the bottom of the editor window to open the panel. Set **Snap Mode** to **Grid Snap** and the **Step** to **64px** in both *x* and *y*. Now, when you click and drag in the texture, it will only allow you to select 64 x 64 sections of the texture:

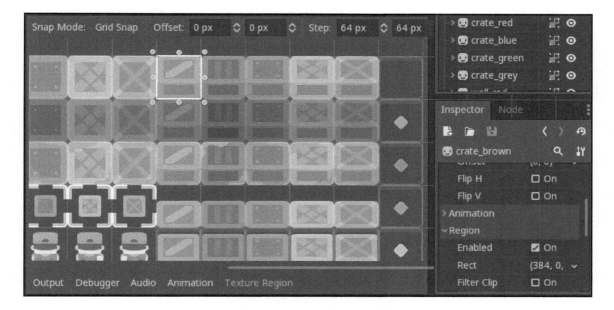

Give the **Sprite** an appropriate name (crate_brown or wall_red, for example)—this name will appear as the tile's name in the TileSet. Add a StaticBody2D as a child, and then add a CollisionPolygon2D to that. It is important that the collision polygon be sized properly so that it aligns with the tiles placed next to it. The easiest way to do this is to turn on grid snapping in the editor window.

Click the **Use Snap** button (it looks like a magnet) and then open the snap menu by clicking on the three dots next to it:

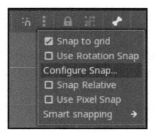

Choose **Configure Snap...** and set the **Grid Step** to 64 by 64:

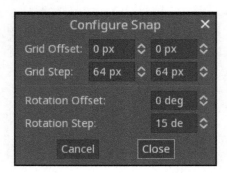

Now, with the CollisionPolygon2D selected, you can click in the four corners of the tile one by one to create a closed square (it will appear as a reddish orange):

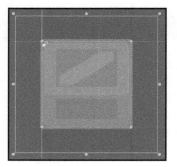

This tile is now complete. You can duplicate it (*Ctrl + D*) and make another, and you only need to change the texture region. Note that collision bodies are only needed on the wall tiles. The ground and item tiles should not have them.

When you've created all your tiles, click **Scene** | **Convert To** | **TileSet** and save it with an appropriate name, such as tileset.tres. If you come back and edit the scene again, you'll need to redo the conversion. Pay special attention to the **Merge With Existing** option. If this is set to **On**, the current scene's tiles will be *merged* with the ones already in the tileset file. Sometimes, this can result in changes to the tile indices and change your map in unwanted ways. Take a look at the following screenshot:

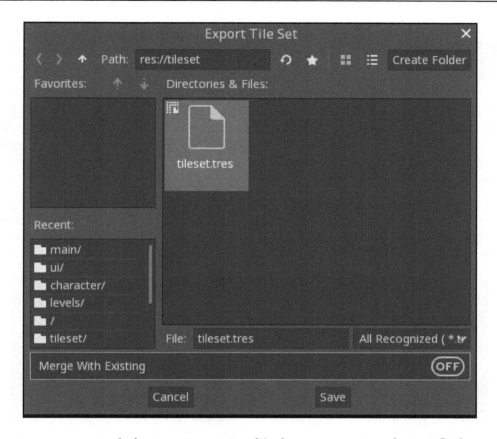

 `tres` stands for text resource and is the most common format Godot stores its resource files in. Compare this with `tscn`, which is the text scene storage format.

Your `TileSet` resource is ready to use!

TileMaps

Now, let's make a new scene for the game level. The level will be a self-contained scene, and will include the map and the player, and will handle spawning any items and enemies in the level. For the root, use a `Node2D` and name it `Level1` (later, you can duplicate this node setup to create more levels).

You can open the Level1.tscn file from the assets folder to see the completed level scene from this section, although you're encouraged to create your own levels.

When using TileMap, you will often want more than one tile object to appear in a given location. You might want to place a tree, for example, but also have a ground tile appear below it. This can be done by using TileMap as many times as you like to create layers of data. For your level, you'll make three layers to display the ground, which the player can walk on; the walls, which are obstacles; and the collectible items, which are markers for spawning items like coins, keys, and enemies.

Add a TileMap and name it Ground. Drag the tileset.tres into the **Tile Set** property and you'll see the tiles appear, ready to be used, on the right-hand side of the editor window:

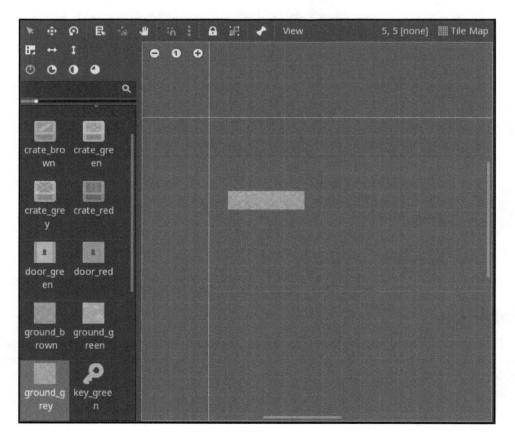

It's very easy to accidentally click and drag in the editor window and move your whole tile map. To prevent this, make sure you select the Ground node and click the Lock button: 🔒.

Duplicate this TileMap twice and name the new TileMap nodes Walls and Items. Remember that Godot draws objects in the order listed in the node tree, from top to bottom, so Ground should be at the top, with Walls and Items underneath it.

As you're drawing your level, be careful to note which layer you're drawing on! You should only place the item markers on the Items layer, for example, because that's where the code is going to look for objects to create. Don't place any other objects there, though, because the layer itself will be invisible during gameplay.

Finally, add an instance of the Player scene. Make sure the Player node is below the three TileMap nodes, so it will be drawn on top. The final scene tree should look like this:

Level script

Now that the level is complete, attach a script to create the level behavior. This script will first scan the Items map to spawn any enemies and collectibles. It will also serve to monitor for events that occur during gameplay, such as picking up a key or running into an enemy:

```
extends Node2D

export (PackedScene) var Enemy
export (PackedScene) var Pickup

onready var items = $Items
var doors = []
```

The first two variables contain references to the scenes that will need to be instanced from the `Items` map. Since that particular map node will be referenced frequently, you can cache the `$Items` lookup in a variable to save some time. Finally, an array called `doors` will contain the door location(s) found on the map.

Save the script and drag the `Enemy.tscn` and `Pickup.tscn` files into their respective properties in the Inspector.

Now, add the following code for `_ready()`:

```
func _ready():
    randomize()
    $Items.hide()
    set_camera_limits()
    var door_id = $Walls.tile_set.find_tile_by_name('door_red')
    for cell in $Walls.get_used_cells_by_id(door_id):
        doors.append(cell)
    spawn_items()
    $Player.connect('dead', self, 'game_over')
    $Player.connect('grabbed_key', self, '_on_Player_grabbed_key')
    $Player.connect('win', self, '_on_Player_win')
```

The function starts by ensuring that the `Items` tilemap is hidden. You don't want the player to see those tiles; they exist so the script can detect where to spawn items.

Next, the camera limits must be set, ensuring that it can't scroll past the edges of the map. You'll create a function to handle that (see the following code).

When the player finds a key, the door(s) need to be opened, so the next part searches the `Walls` map for any `door_red` tiles and stores them in an array. Note that you must first find the tile's `id` from the `TileSet`, because the cells of the `TileMap` only contain ID numbers that refer to the tile set.

More on the `spawn_items()` function follows.

Finally, the `Player` signals are all connected to functions that will process their results.

Here's how to set the camera limits to match the size of the map:

```
func set_camera_limits():
    var map_size = $Ground.get_used_rect()
    var cell_size = $Ground.cell_size
    $Player/Camera2D.limit_left = map_size.position.x * cell_size.x
    $Player/Camera2D.limit_top = map_size.position.y * cell_size.y
    $Player/Camera2D.limit_right = map_size.end.x * cell_size.x
    $Player/Camera2D.limit_bottom = map_size.end.y * cell_size.y
```

`get_used_rect()` returns a `Vector2` containing the size of the `Ground` layer in cells. Multiplying this by the `cell_size` gives the total map size in pixels, which is used to set the four limit values on the `Camera` node. Setting these limits ensures you won't see any *dead* space outside the map when you move near the edge.

Now, add the `spawn_items()` function:

```
func spawn_items():
    for cell in items.get_used_cells():
        var id = items.get_cellv(cell)
        var type = items.tile_set.tile_get_name(id)
        var pos = items.map_to_world(cell) + items.cell_size/2
        match type:
            'slime_spawn':
                var s = Enemy.instance()
                s.position = pos
                s.tile_size = items.cell_size
                add_child(s)
            'player_spawn':
                $Player.position = pos
                $Player.tile_size = items.cell_size
            'coin', 'key_red', 'star':
                var p = Pickup.instance()
                p.init(type, pos)
                add_child(p)
```

This function looks for the tiles in the `Items` layer, returned by `get_used_cells()`. Each cell has an `id` that maps to a name in the `TileSet` (the names that were assigned to each tile when the `TileSet` was made). If you made your own tile set, make sure you use the names that match your tiles in this function. The names used in the preceding code match the tile set that was included in the asset download.

`map_to_world()` converts the tile map position to pixel coordinates. This gives you the upper-left corner of the tile, so then you must add one half-size tile to find the center of the tile. Then, depending on what tile was found, the matching item object is instanced.

Finally, add the three functions for the player signals:

```
func game_over():
    pass

func _on_Player_win():
    pass
```

```
func _on_Player_grabbed_key():
    for cell in doors:
        $Walls.set_cellv(cell, -1)
```

The player signals `dead` and `win` should end the game and go to a **Game Over** screen (which you haven't created yet). Since you can't write the code for those functions yet, use `pass` for the time being. The key pickup signal should remove any door tiles (by setting their tile index to −1, which means an empty tile).

Adding more levels

If you want to make another level, you just need to duplicate this scene tree and attach the same script to it. The easiest way to do this is to use **Scene | Save As** and save the level as `Level2.tscn`. Then, you can use some of the existing tiles or draw a whole new level layout.

Feel free to do this with as many levels as you like, making sure to save them all in the `levels` folder. In the next section, you'll see how to link them together so that each level will lead to the next. Don't worry if you number them incorrectly; you'll be able to put them in whatever order you like.

Game flow

Now that you have the basic building blocks completed, you need to tie everything together. In this section, you'll create:

- The Start and Game Over screens
- A global script to manage persistent data

The basic flow of the game follows the following chart:

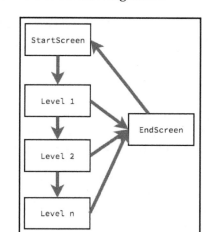

The player is sent to the end screen whenever he/she dies, or when they reach and complete the last level. After a brief time, the end screen returns the player to the start screen so that a new game can be played.

Start and end screens

You need two scenes for this part: a start or title screen that shows before the game (and lets the player start the game), and a game over screen to notify the player that the game has ended.

Make a new scene and add a `Control` node named `StartScreen`. Add a **Label** as a child and add `res://assets/Unique.ttf` as a new `DynamicFont` with a font size of `64`. Set the **Align** and **Valign** properties to **Center** and the **Text** to `Escape the Maze!`. In the **Layout** menu, select **Full Rect**. Now, duplicate this node and set the second label's **Text** to **Press <space>**.

For this demonstration, the `StartScreen` is being kept very plain. Once you have it working, feel free to add decorations, or even an `AnimationPlayer` to make a player Sprite run across the screen.

Choose **Scene** | **Save As** to save another copy of this scene and name it `EndScreen`. Delete the second `Label` (the one that says **Press <space>**) and add a `Timer` node. Set the **Autostart** property to **On, One Shot** to **On**, and **Wait Time** to `3`.

The `Timer` will send the game back to the `StartScreen` after it expires.

However, before you can connect these other scenes together, you need to understand how to work with persistent data and *Autoloads*.

Globals

It is a very common scenario in game development that you have some data that needs to persist across multiple scenes. Data that is part of a scene is lost when the scene is switched, so persistent data must reside somewhere outside the current scene.

Godot solves this problem with the use of AutoLoads. These are scripts or nodes that are automatically loaded in every scene. Because Godot does not support global variables, an autoload acts like a *Singleton*. This is a node (with attached script) that is automatically loaded in *every* scene. Common uses for AutoLoads include storing global data (score, player data, and so on), handling scene switching functions, or any other functions that need to be independent of the currently running scene.

Singleton is a well-known pattern in programming which describes a class that only allows for a single instance of itself, and provides direct access to its member variables and functions. In game development, it is often used for persistent data that needs to be accessible by various parts of the game.

When deciding if you need a singleton, ask yourself whether the object or data needs to *always* exist and if there will always be *only one* instance of that object.

Global script

First, make a new script by clicking **File | New** in the **Script** window. Make sure it inherits from `Node` (this is the default), and in the `Path` field, set the name to `Global.gd`. Click **Create** and add the following code to the new script:

```
extends Node

var levels = ['res://levels/Level1.tscn',
              'res://levels/Level2.tscn']
var current_level

var start_screen = 'res://ui/StartScreen.tscn'
var end_screen = 'res://ui/EndScreen.tscn'
```

```
func new_game():
    current_level = -1
    next_level()

func game_over():
    get_tree().change_scene(end_screen)

func next_level():
    current_level += 1
    if current_level >= Global.levels.size():
        # no more levels to load :(
        game_over()
    else:
        get_tree().change_scene(levels[current_level])
```

This script provides a number of functions you'll need.

Most of the work is done by the `change_scene()` method of the `SceneTree`. The `SceneTree` represents the foundation of the currently running scene. When a scene is loaded or a new node is added, it becomes a member of the `SceneTree`. `change_scene()` replaces the current scene with a given one.

The `next_level()` function progresses through the list of levels you've made, which are listed in the `levels` array. If you reach the end of the list, the game ends.

To add this script as an autoload, open **Project Settings** and click on the **AutoLoad** tab. Click the **..** button next to **Path** and select your `Global.gd` script. The node **Name** will automatically be set to **Global** (this is the name you'll use to reference the node in your scripts, as shown in the following screenshot):

Now, you can access any of the global script's properties by using its name in any script across your whole game, for example, `Global.current_level`.

Attach the following script to the `StartScreen`:

```
extends Control

func _input(event):
    if event.is_action_pressed('ui_select'):
        Global.new_game()
```

This script waits for the spacebar to be pressed and then calls the `new_game()` function of `Global`.

Add this one to `EndScreen`:

```
extends Control

func _on_Timer_timeout():
    get_tree().change_scene(Global.start_screen)
```

You'll also need to connect the `timeout` signal of `Timer`. To do this, you have to create the script first, then the `Connect` button will create the new function for you.

In the `Level.gd` script, you can now fill in the remaining two functions:

```
func _on_Player_win():
    Global.next_level()

func game_over():
    Global.game_over()
```

Score

The global singleton is a great place to keep the player's score so that it will be persistent from level to level. Start by adding a `var score` variable at the top of the file, and then in `new_game()`, add `score = 0`.

Now, you need to add a point whenever a coin is collected. Go to `Pickup.gd` and add `signal coin_pickup` at the top. You can emit this signal in the `pickup()` function:

```
func pickup():
    match type:
        'coin':
            emit_signal('coin_pickup', 1)
    $CollisionShape2D.disabled = true
    $Tween.start()
```

The value of `1` is included here in case you want to later change the number of points that coins are worth, or add other objects that add different point amounts. This signal will be used to update the display, so now you can create the HUD.

Make a new scene with a `CanvasLayer` named HUD and save the scene. Add a `MarginContainer` node as a child, and under that, a `Label` named `ScoreLabel`.

Set the `MarginContainer` **Layout** to **Top Wide** and its four margin properties (found under **Custom Constants**) all to 20. Add the same **Custom Font** properties you used before for the start and end screens, then attach a script:

```
extends CanvasLayer

func _ready():
    $MarginContainer/ScoreLabel.text = str(Global.score)

func update_score(value):
    Global.score += value
    $MarginContainer/ScoreLabel.text = str(Global.score)
```

Add an instance of the HUD to the Level scene. Remember from the previous project that the `CanvasLayer` node will remain on top of the rest of the game. It will also ignore any camera movement, so the display will remain fixed in place as the player moves around the level.

Finally, in the `Level.gd` script, when you spawn a new collectible object, connect the signal to the HUD function:

```
'coin', 'key_red', 'star':
    var p = Pickup.instance()
    p.init(type, pos)
    add_child(p)
    p.connect('coin_pickup', $HUD, 'update_score')
```

Run the game and collect a few coins to confirm that the score is updating.

Saving the High Score

Many games require you to save some kind of information between play sessions. This is information that you want to remain available, even when the application itself has quit. Examples include saved games, user-created content, or downloadable resource packs. For this game, you'll save a High Score value that will persist across game sessions.

Reading and writing files

As you've seen before, Godot keeps all resources stored as files in the project folder. From code, these are accessible under the res:// folder path. For example, res://project.godot will always point to the current project's configuration file, no matter where on your computer the project is actually stored.

However, the res:// filesystem is set as read-only for safety when the project is run. It is also read-only when the project is exported. Any data that needs to be retained by the user is placed in the user:// file path. Where this folder physically exists will vary depending on what platform the game is running on.

 You can find the current platform's user-writable data folder using OS.get_user_data_dir(). Add a print() statement to the ready() function of one of your scripts to see what the location is on your system.

Reading and writing to files is accomplished using a File object. This object is used to open the file in read and/or write mode, and can also be used to test for a file's existence.

Add the following code to Global.gd:

```
var highscore = 0
var score_file = "user://highscore.txt"

func setup():
    var f = File.new()
    if f.file_exists(score_file):
        f.open(score_file, File.READ)
        var content = f.get_as_text()
        highscore = int(content)
        f.close()
```

You first need to test whether the file exists. If it does, you can read the value, which is being stored as human-readable text, and assign it to the highscore variable. Binary data can also be stored in files, if needed, but text will allow you to look at the file yourself and check that everything is working.

Add the following code to check if the player has beat the previous high score:

```
func game_over():
    if score > highscore:
        highscore = score
        save_score()
    get_tree().change_scene(end_screen)

func save_score():
    var f = File.new()
    f.open(score_file, File.WRITE)
    f.store_string(str(highscore))
    f.close()
```

The save_score() function opens the file to write the new value. Note that if the file doesn't exist, opening in WRITE mode will automatically create it.

Next, you need to call the setup() function when the game starts, so add this to Global.gd:

```
func _ready():
    setup()
```

Finally, to display the high score, add another Label node to the StartScreen scene (you can duplicate one of the existing ones). Arrange it below the other Labels (or in whatever order you like) and name it ScoreNotice. Add the following to the script:

```
func _ready():
    $ScoreNotice.text = "High Score: " + str(Global.highscore)
```

Run the game and check that your high score is increasing (when you beat it) and persisting when you quit and start the game again.

Finishing touches

Now that the main functionality of the game is complete, you can add a few more features to polish it up a little bit.

Death animation

When the enemy hits the player, you can add a small animation rather than just ending the game. The effect will spin the character around while shrinking its scale property.

Start by selecting the `AnimationPlayer` node of the `Player` and clicking the **New**

Animation button: . Name the new animation `die`.

In this animation, you'll be animating the Sprite's **Rotation Degrees** and **Scale** properties.

Find the **Rotation Degrees** property in the **Inspector** and click the key, ▬○, to add a track. Move the scrubber to the end of the animation, change **Rotation Degrees** to **360**, and click the key again. Try playing the animation to see the character spin.

> **TIP**
> Keep in mind that while degrees are typically used for Inspector properties, when writing code most Godot functions expect angles to be measured in *radians*.

Now, do the same thing with the *Scale* property. Add a keyframe (at the beginning!) for (1, 1) and then another at the end with the scale set to (0.2, 0.2). Try playing the animation again to see the results.

The new animation needs to be triggered when the player hits an enemy. Add the following code to the player's `_on_Player_area_entered()` function:

```
if area.is_in_group('enemies'):
    area.hide()
    set_process(false)
    $CollisionShape2D.disabled = true
    $AnimationPlayer.play("die")
    yield($AnimationPlayer, 'animation_finished')
    emit_signal('dead')
```

The added code takes care of a few things that need to happen. First, hiding the enemy that was hit makes sure that it doesn't cover the player and prevent you from seeing our new animation. Next, you use `set_process(false)` to stop the `_process()` function from running so that the player can't keep moving during the animation. You also need to disable the player's collision detection so that it doesn't detect another enemy if it happens to wander by.

After starting the `die` animation, you need to let it finish before emitting the `dead` signal, so `yield` is used to wait for the signal from `AnimationPlayer`.

Try running the game and getting hit by an enemy to see the animation. If everything works fine, you'll notice something wrong on the next playthrough: the player is tiny! The animation ends with the Sprite's **Scale** set to (0.2, 0.2) and nothing is setting it back to normal size. Add the following to the Player's script so that the scale will always start at the right value:

```
func _ready():
    $Sprite.scale = Vector2(1, 1)
```

Sound effects

There are six sound effects in the `res://assets/audio` folder for you to use in the game. These audio files are in OGG format. By default, Godot sets OGG files to loop when imported. Select the OGG files in the **FileSystem** tab (you can use *Shift* + Click to select multiple files) and click the **Import** tab on the right-hand side of the editor window. Uncheck **Loop** and click the **Reimport** button:

First, add the pickup sounds for the items. Add two `AudioStreamPlayer` nodes to the `Pickup` scene and name them `KeyPickup` and `CoinPickup`. Drag the corresponding audio file into the **Stream** property of each node.

You can also adjust the sound's volume via its **Volume Db** property, as shown in the following screenshot:

Add the following code to the beginning of the `pickup()` function:

```
match type:
    'coin':
        emit_signal('coin_pickup', 1)
        $CoinPickup.play()
    'key_red':
        $KeyPickup.play()
```

The other sound effects will be added to the Player scene. Add three of the `AudioStreamPlayer` and name them `Win`, `Lose`, and `Footsteps`, adding the matching sound file to each node's **Stream**. Update the `_on_Player_area_entered()` function as follows:

```
if area.type == 'star':
    $Win.play()
    $CollisionShape2D.disabled = true
    yield($Win, "finished")
    emit_signal('win')
```

You need to disable the collision and `yield` for the sound to finish, or else it would be instantly terminated by the next level loading. This way, the player has time to hear the sound before moving on.

To play the footsteps, add `$Footsteps.play()` after `if move(dir):` in the `_process()` function. Note: you may want to reduce the sound of the footsteps so that they don't overwhelm everything; they should be subtle background sounds. In the `Footsteps` node, set the **Volume Db** property to `-30`.

Finally, to play the `Lose` sound, add it to the enemy collision code here:

```
if area.is_in_group('enemies'):
    area.hide()
    $CollisionShape2D.disabled = true
    set_process(false)
    $Lose.play()
    $AnimationPlayer.play("die")
    yield($Lose, 'finished')
    emit_signal('dead')
```

Note that you need to change the yield function. Since the sound is slightly longer than the animation, it will get cut off if you end it on the animation's completion. Alternatively, you could adjust the duration of the animation to match the length of the sound.

Summary

In this project, you have learned how to take advantage of Godot's inheritance system to organize and share code between different objects in your game. This is a very powerful tool that you should keep in mind whenever you start building a new game. If you start making multiple objects that repeat the same properties and/or code, you should probably stop and think about what you're doing. Ask yourself: *can I use inheritance here to share what these objects have in common?* In a bigger game with many more objects, this can save you a large amount of time.

You saw how the `TileMap` node works and how it allows you to quickly design maps and spawn new objects. They have many uses across many game genres. As you'll see later in this book, TileMaps are also ideal for designing platform game levels as well.

You were also introduced to the *AutoLoad* feature, which allows you to create a global script that contains persistent data used across multiple scenes. You also learned how to implement grid-based movement and used the `AnimationPlayer` to work with spritesheet animations.

In the next chapter, you'll learn about Godot's powerful physics body: the `RigidBody2D`. You'll use it to create a game in a classic genre: the space shooter.

4
Space Rocks

By now, you should be getting more comfortable with working in Godot; adding nodes, creating scripts, modifying properties in the **Inspector**, and so on. As you progress through this book, you won't be forced to rehash the basics again and again. If you find yourself stuck, or feeling like you don't quite remember how something is done, feel free to jump back to a previous project where it was explained in more detail. As you repeat the more common actions in Godot, they will start to feel more and more familiar. At the same time, each chapter will introduce you to more nodes and techniques to expand your understanding of Godot's features.

In this next project, you'll make a space shooter game similar to the arcade classic Asteroids. The player will control a ship that can rotate and move in any direction. The goal will be to avoid the floating *space rocks* and shoot them with the ship's laser. Refer to the following screenshot:

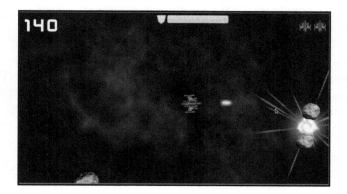

You will learn about the following key topics in this project:

- Physics using `RigidBody2D`
- Finite State Machines
- Building a dynamic, scalable UI
- Sound and music
- Particle effects

Project setup

Create a new project and download the project assets from `https://github.com/` `PacktPublishing/Godot-Game-Engine-Projects/releases`.

For this project, you'll set up custom input actions using the **Input Map**. Using this feature, you can define custom events and assign different keys, mouse events, or other inputs to them. This allows for more flexibility in designing your game, as your code can be written to respond to the `jump` input, for example, without needing to know exactly what input the user pressed to make the event happen. This allows you to make the same code work on different devices, even if they have different hardware. In addition, since many gamers expect to be able to customize a game's inputs, this enables you to provide that option to the user as well.

To set up the inputs for this game, open **Project | Project Settings** and select the **Input Map** tab.

You'll need to create four new input actions: `rotate_left`, `rotate_right`, `thrust`, and `shoot`. Type the name of each action into the **Action** box and click **Add**. Then, for each action, click the + button and select the type of input to assign. For example, to allow the player to use both the arrow keys and the popular WASD alternative, the setup will look like this:

If you have a gamepad or other controller connected to your computer, you can also add its inputs to the actions in the same way. Note: we're only considering button-style inputs at this stage, so while you'll be able to use a d-pad for this project, using an analog joystick would require changes to the project's code.

Rigid body physics

In game development, you often need to know when two objects in the game space intersect or come into contact. This is known as *collision detection*. When a collision is detected, you typically want something to happen. This is known as *collision response*.

Godot offers three kinds of physics bodies, grouped under the `PhysicsBody2D` object type:

- `StaticBody2D`: A static body is one that is not moved by the physics engine. It participates in collision detection, but does not move in response to the collision. This type of body is most often used for objects that are part of the environment or do not need to have any dynamic behavior, such as walls or the ground.

- `RigidBody2D`: This is the physics body in Godot that provides simulated physics. This means that you don't control a `RigidBody2D` directly. Instead, you apply forces to it (gravity, impulses, and so on) and Godot's built-in physics engine calculates the resultant movement, including collisions, bouncing, rotating, and other effects.

- `KinematicBody2D`: This body type provides collision detection, but no physics. All movement must be implemented in code, and you must implement any collision response yourself. Kinematic bodies are most often used for player characters or other actors that require *arcade-style* physics rather than realistic simulation.

Understanding when to use a particular physics body type is a big part of building your game. Using the right node can simplify your development, while trying to force the wrong node to do the job can lead to frustration and poor results. As you work with each type of body, you'll come to learn their pros and cons and get a feel for when they can help build what you need.

In this project, you'll be using the `RigidBody2D` node for the player ship as well as the *space rocks* themselves. You'll learn about the other body types in later chapters.

Individual `RigidBody2D` nodes have many properties you can use to customize their behavior, such as `Mass`, `Friction`, or `Bounce`. These properties can be set in the **Inspector**:

Rigid bodies are also affected by the world's properties, which can be set in the **Project Settings** under **Physics | 2D**. These settings apply to all bodies in the world. Refer to the following screenshot:

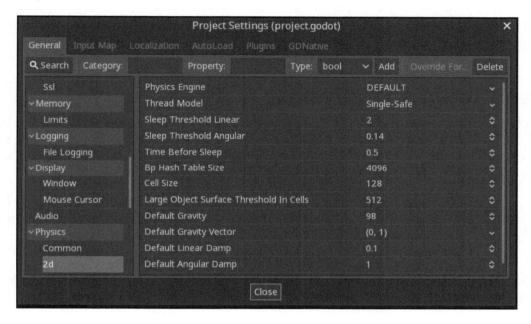

In most cases, you won't need to modify these settings. However, note that by default, gravity has a value of 98 and a direction of (0, 1) (downward). If you want to change the world gravity, you can do that here. You should also be aware of the last two properties, **Default Linear Damp** and **Default Angular Damp**. These properties control how quickly a body will lose forward speed and rotation speed, respectively. Setting them to lower values will make the world feel frictionless, while using larger values will feel like your objects are moving through mud.

 Area2D nodes can also be used to affect rigid body physics by using the **Space Override** property. Custom gravity and damping values will then be applied to any bodies that enter the area.

Since this game will be taking place in outer space, gravity won't be needed, so set **Default Gravity** to 0. You can leave the other settings as they are.

Player ship

The player ship is the heart of the game. Most of the code you'll write for this project will be about making the ship work. It will be controlled in the classic Asteroids style, with left/right rotation and forward thrust. It will also detect the shoot input to allow the player to fire the laser and destroy the floating rocks.

Body setup and physics

Create a new scene and add a `RigidBody2D` named `Player` as the root node, with `Sprite` and `CollisionShape2D` children. Add the `res://assets/player_ship.png` image to the **Texture** property of the `Sprite`. The ship image is quite large, so set the **Scale** property of the `Sprite` to `(0.5, 0.5)` and its **Rotation** to `90`.

> The image for the ship is drawn pointing upwards. In Godot, a rotation of `0` degrees points to the right (along the *x* axis). This means you need to set the **Rotation** of the `Sprite` node to `90` so it will match the body's direction.

In the **Shape** property of `CollisionShape2D`, add a `CircleShape2D` and scale it to cover the image as closely as possible (remember not to move the rectangular size handles):

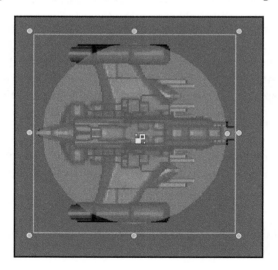

Save the scene. When working on larger-scale projects, it is recommended to organize your scenes and scripts into folders based on each game object. For example, if you make a `player` folder, you can save player-related files there. This makes it easier to find and modify your files rather than having them all together in a single folder. While this project is relatively small, it's a good habit to adopt as your projects grow in size and complexity.

State machines

The player ship can be in a number of different states during gameplay. For example, when *alive*, the ship is visible and can be controlled by the player, but is vulnerable to being hit by rocks. On the other hand, when *invulnerable*, the ship should appear semi-transparent and immune to damage.

One way that programmers often handle situations like this is to add Boolean flag variables to the code. For example, the `invulnerable` flag is set to `true` when the player spawns, or when the `alive` flag is set to `false` when the player is dead. However, this can lead to errors and strange situations where both the `alive` and `invulnerable` flags are set to `true` at the same time. What happens when a rock hits the player in this situation? The two states are mutually exclusive, so this shouldn't be allowed to happen.

One solution to this problem is to use a **Finite State Machine** (**FSM**). When using an FSM, an entity can only be in one state at a given time. To design your FSM, you define some number of states and what events or actions can cause a transition from one state to another.

The following diagram outlines the FSM for the player ship:

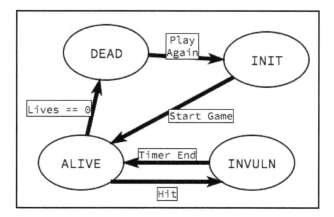

There are four states, and the arrows indicate what transitions are allowed, as well as what event triggers the transition. By checking the current state, you can decide what the player is allowed to do. For example, in the **DEAD** state, don't allow input, or in the **INVULNERABLE** state, don't allow shooting.

Advanced FSM implementations can become quite complex, and the details are beyond the scope of this book (see the Appendix for further reading). In the purest sense, you technically won't be creating a true FSM, but for the purposes of this project, it will be sufficient to illustrate the concept and keep you from running into the Boolean flag problem.

Add a script to the Player node and start by creating the skeleton of the FSM implementation:

```
extends RigidBody2D

enum {INIT, ALIVE, INVULNERABLE, DEAD}
var state = null
```

An enum (short for enumeration) is a convenient way to create a set of constants. The enum statement in the preceding code snippet is equivalent to the following code:

```
const INIT = 0
const ALIVE = 1
const INVULNERABLE = 2
const DEAD = 3
```

You can also assign a name to an enum, which is useful when you have more than one collection of constants in a single script. For example:

```
enum States {INIT, ALIVE}

var state = States.INIT
```

However, this isn't needed in this script, as you'll only be using the one enum to track the ship's states.

Next, create the change_state function to handle state transitions:

```
func _ready():
    change_state(ALIVE)

func change_state(new_state):
    match new_state:
        INIT:
            $CollisionShape2D.disabled = true
```

```
    ALIVE:
        $CollisionShape2D.disabled = false
    INVULNERABLE:
        $CollisionShape2D.disabled = true
    DEAD:
        $CollisionShape2D.disabled = true
state = new_state
```

Whenever you need to change the state of the player, you'll call the
change_state() function and pass it the value of the new state. Then, by using a match
statement, you can execute whatever code should accompany the transition to the new
state. To illustrate this, the CollisionShape2D is being enabled/disabled by the
new_state value. In _ready(), you specify the initial state—currently ALIVE so that you
can test, but you'll change it to INIT later.

Controls

Add the following variables to the script:

```
export (int) var engine_power
export (int) var spin_power

var thrust = Vector2()
var rotation_dir = 0
```

engine_power and spin_power control how fast the ship can accelerate and turn. In the
Inspector, set them to 500 and 15000, respectively. thrust will represent the force being
applied by the ship's engine: either (0, 0) when coasting, or a vector with the length of
engine_power when powered on. rotation_dir will represent what direction the ship is
turning in and apply a torque, or rotational force.

By default, the physics settings provide some *damping*, which reduces a body's velocity and
spin. In space, there's no friction, so for realism there shouldn't be any damping at all.
However, for an arcade-style feel, it's preferable that the ship should stop when you let go
of the keys. In the **Inspector**, set the player's **Linear/Damp** to 1 and its **Angular/Damp** to 5.

The next step is to detect the input and move the ship:

```
func _process(delta):
    get_input()

func get_input():
    thrust = Vector2()
    if state in [DEAD, INIT]:
```

```
            return
    if Input.is_action_pressed("thrust"):
        thrust = Vector2(engine_power, 0)
    rotation_dir = 0
    if Input.is_action_pressed("rotate_right"):
        rotation_dir += 1
    if Input.is_action_pressed("rotate_left"):
        rotation_dir -= 1

func _physics_process(delta):
    set_applied_force(thrust.rotated(rotation))
    set_applied_torque(spin_power * rotation_dir)
```

The `get_input()` function captures the key actions and sets the ship's thrust on or off, and the rotation direction (`rotation_dir`) to a positive or negative value (representing clockwise or counter-clockwise rotation). This function is called every frame in `_process()`. Note that if the state is `INIT` or `DEAD`, `get_input()` will exit by using `return` before checking for key actions.

When using physics bodies, their movement and related functions should be called in `_physics_process()`. Here, you can use `set_applied_force()` to apply the engine thrust in whatever direction the ship is facing. Then, you can use `set_applied_torque()` to cause the ship to rotate.

Play the scene and you should be able to fly around freely.

Screen wrap

Another feature of classic 2D arcade games is *screen wrap*. If the player goes off one side of the screen, they *appear* on the other side. In practice, you teleport or instantaneously change the ship's position to the opposite side. Add the following to the class variables at the top of the script:

```
var screensize = Vector2()
```

And add this to `_ready()`:

```
screensize = get_viewport().get_visible_rect().size
```

Later, the game's main script will handle setting `screensize` for all of the game's objects, but for now, this will allow you to test the screen wrapping with just the player scene.

When first approaching this problem, you might think you could use the body's `position` property and, if it exceeds the bounds of the screen, set it to the opposite side. However, when using `RigidBody2D`, you can't directly set its `position`, because that would conflict with the movement that the physics engine is calculating. A common mistake is to try adding something like this to `_physics_process()`:

```
func _physics_process(delta):
    if position.x > screensize.x:
        position.x = 0
    if position.x < 0:
        position.x = screensize.x
    if position.y > screensize.y:
        position.y = 0
    if position.y < 0:
        position.y = screensize.y
    set_applied_force(thrust.rotated(rotation))
    set_applied_torque(rotation_dir * spin_thrust)
```

This will fail, trapping the player on the edge of the screen (and occasionally *glitching* unpredictably at the corners). So, why doesn't this work? The Godot documentation recommends `_physics_process()` for physics-related code—it even has *physics* in the name. It makes sense at first glance that this should work correctly.

In fact, the correct way to solve this problem is *not* to use `_physics_process()`.

To quote the `RigidBody2D` docs:

> *"You should not change a RigidBody2D's position or linear_velocity every frame or even very often. If you need to directly affect the body's state, use _integrate_forces, which allows you to directly access the physics state."*

And in the description for `_integrate_forces()`:

> *"(It) Allows you to read and safely modify the simulation state for the object. Use this instead of _physics_process if you need to directly change the body's position or other physics properties. (emphasis added)"*

The answer is to change the physics callback to `_integrate_forces()`, which gives you access to the body's `Physics2DDirectBodyState`. This is a Godot object containing a great deal of useful information about the current physics state of the body. In the case of location, the key piece of information is the body's `Transform2D`.

A *transform* is a matrix representing one or more transformations in 2D space such as translation, rotation, and/or scaling. The translation (that is, position) information is found by accessing the `origin` property of the `Transform2D`.

Using this information, you can implement the wrap around effect by changing `_physics_process()` to `_integrate_forces()` and altering the transform's origin:

```
func _integrate_forces(physics_state):
    set_applied_force(thrust.rotated(rotation))
    set_applied_torque(spin_power * rotation_dir)
    var xform = physics_state.get_transform()
    if xform.origin.x > screensize.x:
        xform.origin.x = 0
    if xform.origin.x < 0:
        xform.origin.x = screensize.x
    if xform.origin.y > screensize.y:
        xform.origin.y = 0
    if xform.origin.y < 0:
        xform.origin.y = screensize.y
    physics_state.set_transform(xform)
```

Note that the function's argument name has been changed to `physics_state` from its default: `state`. This is to prevent any possible confusion with the already existing `state` variable, which tracks what FSM state the player is currently assigned to.

Run the scene again and check that everything is working as expected. Make sure you try wrapping around in all four directions. A common mistake is to accidentally flip a greater-than or less-than sign, so check that first if you're having a problem with one or more screen edges.

Shooting

Now, it's time to give your ship some weapons. When pressing the `shoot` action, a bullet should be spawned at the front of the ship and travel in a straight line until it exits the screen. Then, the gun isn't allowed to fire again until a small amount of time has passed.

Bullet scene

This is the node setup for the bullet:

- `Area2D` (named `Bullet`)
- `Sprite`

- CollisionShape2D
- VisibilityNotifier2D

Use res://assets/laser.png from the assets folder for the texture of the Sprite, and a CapsuleShape2D for the collision shape. You'll have to set the **Rotation** of the CollisionShape2D to 90 so that it will fit correctly. You should also scale the Sprite down to half size ((0.5, 0.5)).

Add the following script to the Bullet node:

```
extends Area2D

export (int) var speed
var velocity = Vector2()

func start(pos, dir):
    position = pos
    rotation = dir
    velocity = Vector2(speed, 0).rotated(dir)

func _process(delta):
    position += velocity * delta
```

Set the exported speed property to 1000.

The VisibilityNotifier2D is a node that can inform you (using signals) whenever a node becomes visible/invisible. You can use this to automatically delete a bullet when it goes off screen. Connect the screen_exited signal of VisibilityNotifier2D and add this:

```
func _on_VisibilityNotifier2D_screen_exited():
    queue_free()
```

Finally, connect the bullet's body_entered signal so that you can detect when the bullet hits a rock. The bullet doesn't need to *know* anything about rocks, just that it has hit something. When you create the rocks, you'll add them to a group called rocks and give them an explode() method:

```
func _on_Bullet_body_entered( body ):
    if body.is_in_group('rocks'):
        body.explode()
        queue_free()
```

Firing bullets

Now, you need instances of the bullet to be created whenever the player fires. However, if you make the bullet a child of the player, then it will move and rotate along with the player instead of moving independently. Instead, the bullet should be added as a child of the main scene. One way to do this would be to use `get_parent().add_child()`, since the Main scene will be the parent of the player when the game is running. However, this would mean you could no longer run the Player scene by itself like you have been doing, because `get_parent()` would produce an error. Or, if in the Main scene you decided to arrange things differently, making the player a child of some other node, the bullet wouldn't be added where you expect.

In general, it is a bad idea to write code that assumes a fixed tree layout. Especially try to avoid using `get_parent()` if at all possible. You may find it difficult to think this way at first, but it will result in a much more modular design and prevent some common mistakes.

Instead, the player will *give* the bullet to the main scene using a signal. In this way, the Player scene doesn't need to *know* anything about how the Main scene is set up, or even if the Main scene exists. Producing the bullet and handing it off is the Player object's only responsibility.

Add a `Position2D` node to the player and name it `Muzzle`. This will mark the *muzzle* of the gun—the location where the bullet will spawn. Set its **Position** to (50, 0) to place it directly in front of the ship.

Next, add a `Timer` node named `GunTimer`. This will provide a *cooldown* to the gun, preventing a new bullet from firing until a certain amount of time has passed. Check the **One Shot** and **Autoplay** boxes.

Add these new variables to the player's script:

```
signal shoot

export (PackedScene) var Bullet
export (float) var fire_rate

var can_shoot = true
```

Drag the `Bullet.tscn` onto the new **Bullet** property in the **Inspector**, and set the **Fire Rate** to 0.25 (this value is in seconds).

Add this to `_ready()`:

```
$GunTimer.wait_time = fire_rate
```

And this to `get_input()`:

```
if Input.is_action_pressed("shoot") and can_shoot:
    shoot()
```

Now, create the `shoot()` function, which will handle creating the bullet(s):

```
func shoot():
    if state == INVULNERABLE:
        return
    emit_signal("shoot", Bullet, $Muzzle.global_position, rotation)
    can_shoot = false
    $GunTimer.start()
```

When emitting the `shoot` signal, you pass the `Bullet` itself plus its starting position and direction. Then, you disable shooting with the `can_shoot` flag and start the `GunTimer`. To allow the gun to shoot again, connect the `timeout` signal of the `GunTimer`:

```
func _on_GunTimer_timeout():
    can_shoot = true
```

Now, make your Main scene. Add a `Node` named `Main` and a `Sprite` named `Background`. Use `res://assets/space_background.png` as the Texture. Add an instance of the `Player` to the scene.

Add a script to `Main`, then connect the `Player` node's `shoot` signal, and add the following to the created function:

```
func _on_Player_shoot(bullet, pos, dir):
    var b = bullet.instance()
    b.start(pos, dir)
    add_child(b)
```

Play the `Main` scene and test that you can fly and shoot.

Rocks

The goal of the game is to destroy the floating space rocks, so, now that you can shoot, it's time to add them. Like the ship, the rocks will also be RigidBody2D, which will make them travel in a straight line at a steady speed unless disturbed. They'll also bounce off each other in a realistic fashion. To make things more interesting, rocks will start out large and, when you shoot them, break into multiple smaller rocks.

Scene setup

Start a new scene by making a RigidBody2D, naming it Rock, and adding a Sprite using the res://assets/rock.png texture. Add a CollisionShape2D, but *don't* add a shape to it yet. Because you'll be spawning different-sized rocks, the collision shape will need to be set in the code and adjusted to the correct size.

Set the **Bounce** property of the Rock to 1 and both **Linear/Damp** and **Angular/Damp** to 0.

Variable size

Attach a script and define the member variables:

```
extends RigidBody2D

var screensize = Vector2()
var size
var radius
var scale_factor = 0.2
```

The Main script will handle spawning new rocks, both at the beginning of a level as well as the smaller rocks that will appear after a large one explodes. A large rock will have a size of 3 and break into rocks of size 2, and so on. The scale_factor is multiplied by size to set the sprite's scale, the collision radius, and so on. You can adjust it later to change how big each category of rock is.

All of this will be set by the start() method:

```
func start(pos, vel, _size):
    position = pos
    size = _size
    mass = 1.5 * size
    $Sprite.scale = Vector2(1, 1) * scale_factor * size
```

```
radius = int($Sprite.texture.get_size().x / 2 * scale_factor * size)
var shape = CircleShape2D.new()
shape.radius = radius
$CollisionShape2D.shape = shape
linear_velocity = vel
angular_velocity = rand_range(-1.5, 1.5)
```

Here is where you calculate the correct collision shape based on the rock's `size` and add it to the `CollisionShape2D`. Note that since `size` is already in use as a class variable, you can use `_size` for the function argument.

The rocks also need to wrap around the screen, so use the same technique you used for the `Player`:

```
func _integrate_forces(physics_state):
    var xform = physics_state.get_transform()
    if xform.origin.x > screensize.x + radius:
        xform.origin.x = 0 - radius
    if xform.origin.x < 0 - radius:
        xform.origin.x = screensize.x + radius
    if xform.origin.y > screensize.y + radius:
        xform.origin.y = 0 - radius
    if xform.origin.y < 0 - radius:
        xform.origin.y = screensize.y + radius
    physics_state.set_transform(xform)
```

The difference here is that including the body's `radius` results in smoother-looking teleportation. The rock will appear to fully exit the screen before entering at the opposite side. You may want to do the same thing with the player ship. Try it and see which effect you like better.

Instancing

When new rocks are spawned, the main scene will need to pick a random start location. To do this, you could use some geometry to pick a random point along the perimeter of the screen, but instead you can take advantage of yet another Godot node type. You'll draw a path around the edge of the screen, and the script will pick a random location along the path. Add a `Path2D` node and name it `RockPath`. When you click on the `Path2D`, you will see some new buttons appear at the top of the editor:

Select the middle one (**Add Point**) to draw the path by clicking to add the points shown. To make the points align, make sure **Snap to grid** is checked. This option is found under the **Snapping Options** button to the left of the `Lock` button. It appears as a series of three vertical dots. Refer to the following screenshot:

Draw the points in the order shown in the following screenshot. After clicking the fourth point, click the **Close Curve** button (**5**) and your path will be complete:

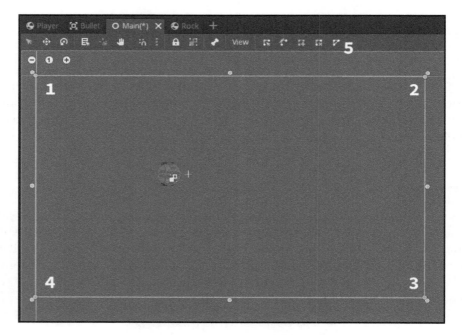

Now that the path is defined, add a `PathFollow2D` node as a child of `RockPath` and name it `RockSpawn`. This node's purpose is to automatically follow a path as it moves, using its `set_offset()` method. The higher the offset, the further along the path it goes. Since our path is closed, it will loop around if the offset value is bigger than the path's length.

Next, add a `Node` and name it `Rocks`. This node will serve as a container to hold all the rocks. By checking its number of children, you can tell if there are any rocks remaining.

Now, add this to `Main.gd`:

```
export (PackedScene) var Rock

func _ready():
    randomize()
    screensize = get_viewport().get_visible_rect().size
    $Player.screensize = screensize
    for i in range(3):
        spawn_rock(3)
```

The script starts by getting the `screensize` and passing that to the `Player`. Then, it spawns three rocks of size 3 using `spawn_rock()`, which is defined in the following code. Don't forget to drag `Rock.tscn` onto the **Rock** property in the **Inspector**:

```
func spawn_rock(size, pos=null, vel=null):
    if !pos:
        $RockPath/RockSpawn.set_offset(randi())
        pos = $RockPath/RockSpawn.position
    if !vel:
        vel = Vector2(1, 0).rotated(rand_range(0, 2*PI)) * rand_range(100,
150)
    var r = Rock.instance()
    r.screensize = screensize
    r.start(pos, vel, size)
    $Rocks.add_child(r)
```

This function will serve two purposes. When called with only a size parameter, it picks a random position along the `RockPath` and a random velocity. However, if those values are also provided, it will use them instead. This will let you spawn the smaller rocks at the location of the explosion.

Run the game and you should see three rocks floating around. However, your bullets don't affect them.

Exploding rocks

The `Bullet` is checking for bodies in the `rocks` group, so in the `Rock` scene, click on the
Node tab and choose **Groups**. Type `rocks` and click **Add**:

Now, if you run the game and shoot a rock, you'll see an error message because the bullet is
trying to call the rock's `explode()` method, which you haven't defined yet. This method
needs to do three things:

- Remove the rock
- Play an explosion animation
- Notify `Main` to spawn new, smaller rocks

Explosion scene

The explosion will be a separate scene, which you can add to the `Rock` and later to
the `Player`. It will contain two nodes:

- `Sprite` (named `Explosion`)
- `AnimationPlayer`

For the sprite's **Texture**, use `res://assets/explosion.png`. You'll notice that this is a
sprite sheet—an image made up of 64 smaller images laid out in a grid pattern. These
images are the individual frames of the animation. You'll often find animations packaged
this way, and Godot's `Sprite` node supports using them as individual frames.

In the Inspector, find the sprite's **Animation** section. Set the **Vframes** and **Hframes** both to 8. This will *slice* the sprite sheet into its individual images. You can verify this by changing the **Frame** property to different values between 0 and 63. Make sure to set **Frames** back to 0 when finished:

The AnimationPlayer can be used to animate any property of any node. You'll use the AnimationPlayer to change the **Frame** property over time. Start by clicking on the node and you'll see the **Animation** panel open at the bottom, as shown in the following screenshot:

Click the **New Animation** button and name it explosion. Set the **Length** to 0.64 and the **Step** to 0.01. Now, click on the Sprite node and you'll notice that each property in the **Inspector** now has a key button next to it. Each time you click on the key, you create a keyframe in the current animation. The key button next to the **Frame** property also has a + symbol on it, indicating that it will automatically increment the value when you add a key frame.

Click the key and confirm that you want to create a new animation track. Note that the **Frame** property has incremented to 1. Click the key button repeatedly until you have reached the final frame (63).

Click the **Play** button in the **Animation** panel to see the animation being played.

Adding to Rock

In the Rock scene, add an instance of Explosion and add this line to start():

```
$Explosion.scale = Vector2(0.75, 0.75) * size
```

This will ensure that the explosion is scaled to match the rock's size.

Add a signal called exploded at the top of the script, then add the explode() function, which will be called when the bullet hits the rock:

```
func explode():
    layers = 0
    $Sprite.hide()
    $Explosion/AnimationPlayer.play("explosion")
    emit_signal("exploded", size, radius, position, linear_velocity)
    linear_velocity = Vector2()
    angular_velocity = 0
```

The layers property ensures that the explosion will be drawn on top of the other sprites on the screen. Then, you will send a signal that will let Main know to spawn new rocks. This signal also needs to pass the necessary data so that the new rocks will have the right properties.

When the animation finishes playing, the `AnimationPlayer` will emit a signal. To connect it, you need to make the `AnimationPlayer` node visible. Right-click on the instanced **Explosion** and select **Editable Children**, then select the `AnimationPlayer` and connect its `animation_finished` signal. Make sure to select the `Rock` in the **Connect to Node** section. The end of the animation means it is safe to delete the rock:

```
func _on_AnimationPlayer_animation_finished( name ):
    queue_free()
```

Now, test the game and check that you can see explosions when you shoot the rocks. At this point, your rock scene should look like this:

Spawning smaller rocks

The `Rock` is emitting the signal, but it needs to be connected in `Main`. You can't use the **Node** tab to connect it, because the `Rock` instances are being created in code. Signals can be connected in code as well. Add this line to the end of `spawn_rock()`:

```
r.connect('exploded', self, '_on_Rock_exploded')
```

This connects the rock's signal to a function in `Main` called `_on_Rock_exploded()`. Create that function, which will be called whenever a rock sends its `exploded` signal:

```
func _on_Rock_exploded(size, radius, pos, vel):
    if size <= 1:
        return
    for offset in [-1, 1]:
        var dir = (pos - $Player.position).normalized().tangent() * offset
        var newpos = pos + dir * radius
        var newvel = dir * vel.length() * 1.1
        spawn_rock(size - 1, newpos, newvel)
```

In this function, two new rocks are created unless the rock that was just destroyed was the smallest size it can be. The `offset` loop variable will ensure that they spawn and travel in opposite directions (that is, one will be the negative of the other). The `dir` variable finds the vector between the player and the rock, then uses `tangent()` to find the perpendicular to that vector. This ensures that the new rocks travel away from the player:

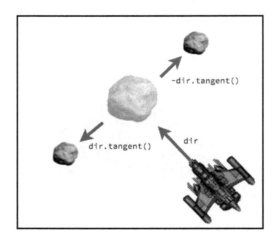

Play the game once again and check that everything is working as expected.

UI

Creating a game UI can be very complex, or at least time-consuming. Precisely placing individual elements and ensuring they work on different-sized screens and devices is the least interesting part of game development for many programmers. Godot provides a wide variety of Control nodes to assist in this process. Learning how to use the various Control nodes will help lessen the pain of creating your game's UI.

For this game, you don't need a very complex UI. The game needs to provide the following information and interactions:

- Start button
- Status message (Get Ready or Game Over)
- Score
- Lives counter

The following is a preview of what you will be able to create:

Create a new scene, and add a CanvasLayer with the name HUD as its root node. The UI will be built on this layer by using Godot's Control **Layout** features.

Layout

Godot's Control nodes include a number of specialized containers. These nodes can be nested inside each other to create the precise layout you need. For example, a MarginContainer will automatically add padding around its contents, while HBoxContainer and VBoxContainer organize their contents in rows or columns, respectively.

Start by adding a MarginContainer, which will hold the score and lives counter. Under the **Layout** menu, select **Top Wide**. Then, scroll down to the **Custom Constants** section and set all four margins to 20.

Next, add an HBoxContainer, which will hold the score counter on the left and the lives counter on the right. Under this container, add a Label (name it ScoreLabel) and another HBoxContainer (name it LivesCounter).

Set the ScoreLabel **Text** to 0 and, under Size Flags, set **Horizontal** to **Fill, Expand**. Under **Custom Fonts**, add a DynamicFont like you did in Chapter 1, *Introduction*, using res://assets/kenvector_future_thin.ttf from the assets folder and setting the size to 64.

Under the `LivesCounter`, add a `TextureRect` and name it `L1`. Drag `res://assets/player_small.png` into the **Texture** property and set the **Stretch Mode** to **Keep Aspect Centered**. Make sure you have the `L1` node selected and press Duplicate (*Ctrl + D*) two times to create `L2` and `L3` (they'll be named automatically). During the game, the `HUD` will show/hide these three textures to indicate how many lives the user has left.

In a larger, more complicated UI, you could save this section as its own scene and embed it in other sections of the UI. However, this game only needs a few more pieces for its UI, so it's fine to combine them all in one scene.

As a child of the `HUD` node, add a `TextureButton` (named `StartButton`), a `Label` (named `MessageLabel`), and a `Timer` (named `MessageTimer`).

In the `res://assets` folder, there are two textures for the `StartButton`, one normal (`play_button.png`) and one to show when the mouse is hovering over it (`play_button_h.png`). Drag these to the **Textures/Normal** and **Textures/Hover** properties, respectively. In the **Layout** menu, choose **Center**.

For the `MessageLabel`, make sure you set the font first before specifying the layout, or it won't be centered properly. You can use the same settings you used for the `ScoreLabel`. After setting the font, set the layout to **Full Rect**.

Finally, set the **One Shot** property of `MessageTimer` to **On** and its **Wait Time** to 2.

When finished, your UI's scene tree should look like this:

UI functions

You've completed the UI layout, so now let's add a script to HUD so you can add the functionality:

```
extends CanvasLayer

signal start_game

onready var lives_counter =
[$MarginContainer/HBoxContainer/LivesCounter/L1,
$MarginContainer/HBoxContainer/LivesCounter/L2,
$MarginContainer/HBoxContainer/LivesCounter/L3]
```

The start_game signal will be emitted when the player clicks the StartButton. The lives_counter variable is an array holding references to the three life counter images. The names are fairly long, so make sure to let the editor's autocomplete fill them in for you to avoid mistakes.

Next, you need functions to handle updating the displayed information:

```
func show_message(message):
    $MessageLabel.text = message
    $MessageLabel.show()
    $MessageTimer.start()

func update_score(value):
    $MarginContainer/MarginContainer/HBoxContainer/ScoreLabel.text =
str(value)

func update_lives(value):
    for item in range(3):
        lives_counter[item].visible = value > item
```

Each function will be called when a value changes to update the display.

Next, add a function to handle the Game Over state:

```
func game_over():
    show_message("Game Over")
    yield($MessageTimer, "timeout")
    $StartButton.show()
```

Now, connect the `pressed` signal of the `StartButton` so that it can emit the signal to `Main`:

```
func _on_StartButton_pressed():
    $StartButton.hide()
    emit_signal("start_game")
```

Finally, connect the `timeout` signal of `MessageTimer` so that it can hide the message:

```
func _on_MessageTimer_timeout():
    $MessageLabel.hide()
    $MessageLabel.text = ''
```

Main scene code

Now, you can add an instance of the `HUD` to the `Main` scene. Add the following variables to `Main.gd`:

```
var level = 0
var score = 0
var playing = false
```

These will track the named quantities. The following code will handle starting a new game:

```
func new_game():
    for rock in $Rocks.get_children():
        rock.queue_free()
    level = 0
    score = 0
    $HUD.update_score(score)
    $Player.start()
    $HUD.show_message("Get Ready!")
    yield($HUD/MessageTimer, "timeout")
    playing = true
    new_level()
```

First, you need to make sure that you remove any existing rocks that are left over from the previous game and initialize the variables. Don't worry about the `start()` function on the player; you'll add that soon.

After showing the `"Get Ready!"` message, you will use `yield` to wait for the message to disappear before actually starting the level:

```
func new_level():
    level += 1
    $HUD.show_message("Wave %s" % level)
    for i in range(level):
        spawn_rock(3)
```

This function will be called every time the level changes. It announces the level number and spawns a number of rocks to match. Note—since you initialized `level` to `0`, this will set it to `1` for the first level.

To detect whether the level has ended, you continually check how many children the `Rocks` node has:

```
func _process(delta):
    if playing and $Rocks.get_child_count() == 0:
        new_level()
```

Now, you need to connect the HUD's `start_game` signal (emitted when the Play button is pressed) to the `new_game()` function. Select the HUD, click on the **Node** tab, and connect the `start_game` signal. Set **Make Function** to **Off** and type `new_game` in the **Method In Node** field.

Next, add the following function to handle what happens when the game ends:

```
func game_over():
    playing = false
    $HUD.game_over()
```

Play the game and check that pressing the Play button starts the game. Note that the `Player` is currently stuck in the `INIT` state, so you can't fly around yet—the `Player` doesn't know the game has started.

Player code

Add a new signal and a new variable to `Player.gd`:

```
signal lives_changed

var lives = 0 setget set_lives
```

The `setget` statement in GDScript allows you to specify a function that will be called whenever the value of a given variable is changed. This means that when `lives` decreases, you can emit a signal to let the `HUD` know it needs to update the display:

```
func set_lives(value):
    lives = value
    emit_signal("lives_changed", lives)
```

The `start()` function is called by `Main` when a new game starts:

```
func start():
    $Sprite.show()
    self.lives = 3
    change_state(ALIVE)
```

 When using `setget`, if you access the variable locally (in the local script), you must put `self.` in front of the variable name. If you don't, the `setget` function will not be called.

Now, you need to connect this signal from the `Player` to the `update_lives` method in the `HUD`. In `Main`, click on the `Player` instance and find its `lives_changed` signal in the **Node** tab. Click **Connect**, and in the connection window, under **Connect to Node**, choose the `HUD`. For **Method In Node**, type `update_lives`. Make sure you have **Make Function** off, and click **Connect**, as shown in the following screenshot:

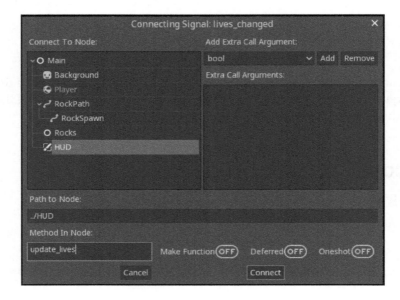

Game over

In this section, you'll make the player detect when it is hit by rocks, add an invulnerability feature, and end the game when the player runs out of lives.

Add an instance of the `Explosion` to the `Player`, as well as a `Timer` node (named `InvulnerabilityTimer`). In the **Inspector**, set the **Wait Time** of `InvulnerabilityTimer` to 2 and its **One Shot** to **On**. Add this to the top of `Player.gd`:

```
signal dead
```

This signal will notify the `Main` scene that the player has run out of lives and the game is over. Before that, however, you need to update the state machine to do a little more with each state:

```
func change_state(new_state):
    match new_state:
        INIT:
            $CollisionShape2D.disabled = true
            $Sprite.modulate.a = 0.5
        ALIVE:
            $CollisionShape2D.disabled = false
            $Sprite.modulate.a = 1.0
        INVULNERABLE:
            $CollisionShape2D.disabled = true
            $Sprite.modulate.a = 0.5
            $InvulnerabilityTimer.start()
        DEAD:
            $CollisionShape2D.disabled = true
            $Sprite.hide()
            linear_velocity = Vector2()
            emit_signal("dead")
    state = new_state
```

The `modulate.a` property of a sprite sets its alpha channel (transparency). Setting it to `0.5` makes it semi-transparent, while `1.0` is solid.

After entering the `INVULNERABLE` state, you start the `InvulnerabilityTimer`. Connect its `timeout` signal:

```
func _on_InvulnerabilityTimer_timeout():
    change_state(ALIVE)
```

Also, connect the `animation_finished` signal from the `Explosion` animation like you did in the `Rock` scene:

```
func _on_AnimationPlayer_animation_finished( name ):
    $Explosion.hide()
```

Detecting collisions between physics bodies

When you fly around, the player ship bounces off the rocks, because both bodies are `RigidBody2D` nodes. However, if you want to make something happen when two rigid bodies collide, you need to enable contact monitoring. Select the `Player` node and in the Inspector, set **Contact Monitoring** to **On**. By default, no contacts are reported, so you must also set **Contacts Reported** to 1. Now, the body will emit a signal when it contacts another body. Click on the **Node** tab and connect the `body_entered` signal:

```
func _on_Player_body_entered( body ):
    if body.is_in_group('rocks'):
        body.explode()
        $Explosion.show()
        $Explosion/AnimationPlayer.play("explosion")
        self.lives -= 1
        if lives <= 0:
            change_state(DEAD)
        else:
            change_state(INVULNERABLE)
```

Now, go to the `Main` scene and connect the Player's `dead` signal to the `game_over()` function. Play the game and try running into a rock. Your ship should explode, become invulnerable (for two seconds), and lose one life. Check that the game ends if you get hit three times.

Pausing the game

Many games require some sort of pause mode to allow the player to take a break in the action. In Godot, pausing is a function of the scene tree and can be set using `get_tree().paused = true`. When the `SceneTree` is paused, three things happen:

- The physics thread stops running

- _process and _physics_process are no longer called, so no code in those methods is run
- _input and _input_event are also not called

When the pause mode is triggered, every node in the running game can react accordingly, based on how you've configured it. This behavior is set via the node's **Pause/Mode** property, which you'll find all the way at the bottom of the Inspector list.

The pause mode can be set to three values: INHERIT (the default value), STOP, and PROCESS. STOP means the node will cease processing while the tree is paused, while PROCESS sets the node to continue running, ignoring the paused state of the tree. Because it would be very tedious to set this property on every node in the whole game, INHERIT lets the node use the same pause mode as its parent.

Open the **Input Map** tab (in **Project Settings**) and create a new input action called pause. Choose a key you'd like to use to toggle pause mode; for example, P is a good choice.

Next, add the following function to Main.gd to respond to the input action:

```
func _input(event):
    if event.is_action_pressed('pause'):
        if not playing:
            return
    get_tree().paused = not get_tree().paused
    if get_tree().paused:
        $HUD/MessageLabel.text = "Paused"
        $HUD/MessageLabel.show()
    else:
        $HUD/MessageLabel.text = ""
        $HUD/MessageLabel.hide()
```

If you ran the game now, you'd have a problem—all nodes are paused, including Main. This means that since it isn't processing _input, it can't detect the input again to unpause the game! To fix this, you need to set the **Pause/Mode** of Main to PROCESS. Now, you have the opposite problem: all the nodes below Main inherit this setting. This is fine for most of the nodes, but you need to set the mode to STOP on these three nodes: Player, Rocks, and HUD.

Enemies

Space is filled with more dangers than just rocks. In this section, you'll create an enemy spaceship that will periodically appear and shoot at the player.

Following a path

When the enemy appears, it should follow a path across the screen. To keep it from looking too repetitive, you can create multiple paths and randomly choose one when the enemy starts.

Create a new scene and add a Node. Name it EnemyPaths and save the scene. To draw the path, add a Path2D node. As you saw earlier, this node allows you to draw a series of connected points. When you add the node, a new menu bar appears:

These buttons let you draw and modify the path's points. Click the one with the + symbol to add points. Click to start the path somewhere just outside the game window (the bluish-purple rectangle), and then click a few more points to create a curve. Don't worry about making it smooth just yet:

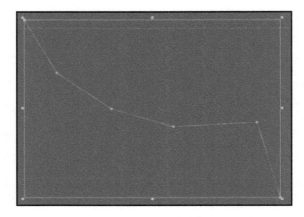

When the enemy ship follows the path, it will not look very smooth when it hits the sharp corners. To smooth the curve, click the second button in the path toolbar (its tooltip says **Select Control Points**). Now, if you click and drag any of the curve's points, you will add a control point that allows you to angle and curve the line. Smoothing the preceding line results in something like this:

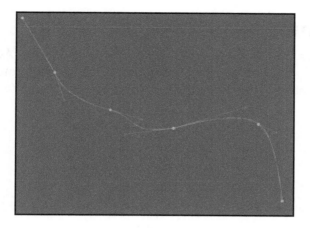

Add a few more `Path2D` nodes to the scene and draw the paths however you like. Adding loops and curves rather than straight lines will make the enemy look more dynamic (and make it harder to hit). Remember that the first point you click will be the start of the path, so make sure to place them on different sides of the screen, for variety. Here are three example paths:

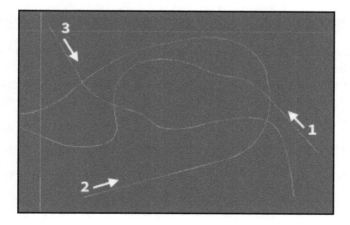

Save the scene. You'll add this to the enemy's scene to give it the paths it can follow.

Enemy scene

Create a new scene for the Enemy, using an `Area2D` as its root node. Add a `Sprite` and use `res://assets/enemy_saucer.png` as its **Texture**. Set the **Animation/HFrames** to 3 so that you can choose between the different-colored ships:

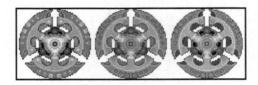

As you've done before, add a `CollisionShape2D` and give it a `CircleShape2D` scaled to cover the sprite image. Next, add an instance of the `EnemyPaths` scene and an `AnimationPlayer`. In the `AnimationPlayer`, you'll need two animations: one to make the saucer spin as it moves, and the other to create a flash effect when the saucer is hit:

- **Rotate animation**: Add a new animation named `rotate` and set its **Length** to 3. Add a keyframe for the `Sprite` **Transform/Rotation Degrees** property after setting it to 0, then drag the play bar to the end and add a keyframe with the rotation set to 360. Click the **Loop** button and the **Autoplay** button.

- **Hit animation**: Add a second animation named `flash`. Set its **Length** to 0.25 and the **Step** to 0.01. The property you'll be animating is the Sprite's **Modulate** (found under **Visibility**). Add a keyframe for **Modulate** to create the track, then move the scrubber to 0.04 and change the **Modulate** color to red. Move forward another 0.04 and change the color back to white.

Repeat this process two more times so that you have three flashes in total.

Add an instance of the `Explosion` scene as you did with the other objects. Also, like you did with the rocks, connect the explosion's `AnimationPlayer` `animation_finished` signal and set it to delete the enemy when the explosion finishes:

```
func _on_AnimationPlayer_animation_finished(anim_name):
    queue_free()
```

Next, add a `Timer` node called `GunTimer` that will control how often the enemy shoots at the player. Set its **Wait Time** to 1.5 and **Autostart** to On. Connect its `timeout` signal, but leave the code reading `pass` for now.

Finally, click on the `Area2D` and the **Node** tab and add it to a group called `enemies`. As with the rocks, this will give you a way to identify the object, even if there are multiple enemies on the screen at the same time.

Moving the Enemy

Attach a script to the `Enemy` scene. To begin, you'll make the code that will select a path and move the enemy along it:

```
extends Area2D

signal shoot

export (PackedScene) var Bullet
export (int) var speed = 150
export (int) var health = 3

var follow
var target = null

func _ready():
    $Sprite.frame = randi() % 3
    var path = $EnemyPaths.get_children()[randi() %
$EnemyPaths.get_child_count()]
    follow = PathFollow2D.new()
    path.add_child(follow)
    follow.loop = false
```

A `PathFollow2D` node is one that can automatically move along a parent `Path2D`. By default, it is set to loop around the path, so you need to manually set the property to `false`.

The next step is to move along the path:

```
func _process(delta):
    follow.offset += speed * delta
    position = follow.global_position
    if follow.unit_offset > 1:
        queue_free()
```

You can detect the end of the path when `offset` is greater than the total path length. However, it's more straightforward to use `unit_offset`, which varies from zero to one over the length of the path.

Spawning enemies

Open the Main scene and add a Timer node called EnemyTimer. Set its **One Shot** property to On. Then, in Main.gd, add a variable to reference your enemy scene (drag it into the **Inspector** after saving the script):

```
export (PackedScene) var Enemy
```

Add the following code to new_level():

```
$EnemyTimer.wait_time = rand_range(5, 10)
$EnemyTimer.start()
```

Connect the EnemyTimer timeout signal, and add the following:

```
func _on_EnemyTimer_timeout():
    var e = Enemy.instance()
    add_child(e)
    e.target = $Player
    e.connect('shoot', self, '_on_Player_shoot')
    $EnemyTimer.wait_time = rand_range(20, 40)
    $EnemyTimer.start()
```

This code instances the enemy whenever the EnemyTimer times out. When you add shooting to the enemy, it will use the same process you used for the Player, so you can reuse the same bullet-spawning function, which is _on_Player_shoot().

Play the game, and you should see a flying saucer appear that will fly along one of your paths.

Enemy shooting and collisions

The enemy needs to shoot at the player as well as react when hit by the player or the player's bullets.

Open the Bullet scene and choose **Save Scene As** to save it as EnemyBullet.tscn (afterwards, don't forget to rename the root node as well). Remove the script by selecting the root node and clicking the **Clear the script** button:

You also need to disconnect the signal connections by clicking the **Node** tab and choosing **Disconnect**:

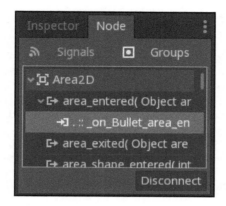

There is also a different texture in the `assets` folder you can use to make the enemy bullet appear distinct from the player's.

The script will be very much the same as the regular bullet. Connect the area's `body_entered` signal and the `screen_exited` signal of `VisibilityNotifier2D`:

```
extends Area2D

export (int) var speed

var velocity = Vector2()

func start(_position, _direction):
    position = _position
    velocity = Vector2(speed, 0).rotated(_direction)
    rotation = _direction

func _process(delta):
    position += velocity * delta

func _on_EnemyBullet_body_entered(body):
    queue_free()

func _on_VisibilityNotifier2D_screen_exited():
    queue_free()
```

For now, the bullet won't do any damage to the player. You'll be adding a shield to the player in the next section, so you can add that at the same time.

Save the scene and drag it into the **Bullet** property on the Enemy.

In Enemy.gd, add the shoot function:

```
func shoot():
    var dir = target.global_position - global_position
    dir = dir.rotated(rand_range(-0.1, 0.1)).angle()
    emit_signal('shoot', Bullet, global_position, dir)
```

First, you must find the vector pointing to the player's position, then add a little bit of randomness to it so that the bullets don't follow exactly the same path.

For an extra challenge, you can make the enemy shoot in *pulses*, or multiple rapid shots:

```
func shoot_pulse(n, delay):
    for i in range(n):
        shoot()
        yield(get_tree().create_timer(delay), 'timeout')
```

This function creates a given number of bullets with delay time between them. You can use this whenever the GunTimer triggers a shot:

```
func _on_GunTimer_timeout():
    shoot_pulse(3, 0.15)
```

This will shoot a pulse of 3 bullets with 0.15 seconds between them. Tough to dodge!

Next, the enemy needs to take damage when it's hit by a shot from the player. It will flash using the animation you made, and then explode when its health reaches 0.

Add these functions to Enemy.gd:

```
func take_damage(amount):
    health -= amount
    $AnimationPlayer.play('flash')
    if health <= 0:
        explode()
    yield($AnimationPlayer, 'animation_finished')
    $AnimationPlayer.play('rotate')

func explode():
    speed = 0
    $GunTimer.stop()
    $CollisionShape2D.disabled = true
```

```
$Sprite.hide()
$Explosion.show()
$Explosion/AnimationPlayer.play("explosion")
$ExplodeSound.play()
```

Also, connect the area's `body_entered` signal so the enemy will explode if the player runs into it:

```
func _on_Enemy_body_entered(body):
    if body.name == 'Player':
        pass
    explode()
```

Again, you're waiting for the player shield to add the damage to the player, so leave the `pass` placeholder there for now.

Right now, the player's bullet is only detecting physics bodies because its `body_entered` signal is connected. However, the enemy is an `Area2D`, so it will not trigger that signal. To detect the enemy, you need to also connect the `area_entered` signal:

```
func _on_Bullet_area_entered(area):
    if area.is_in_group('enemies'):
        area.take_damage(1)
    queue_free()
```

Try playing the game again and you'll be doing battle with an aggressive alien opponent! Verify that all the collision combinations are being handled. Also note that the enemy's bullets can be blocked by rocks—maybe you can hide behind them for cover!

Additional features

The structure of the game is complete. You can start the game, play it through, and when it ends, play again. In this section, you'll add some additional effects and features to the game to improve the gameplay experience. Effects is a broad term and can mean many different techniques, but in this case, you'll specifically address three things:

- **Sound effects and music:** Audio is very often overlooked, but can be a very effective part of game design. Good sound improves the *feel* of the game. Bad or annoying sounds can create boredom or frustration. You'll add some action-packed background music, and some sound effects for several actions in the game.

- **Particles:** Particle effects are images, usually small, that are generated in large numbers and animated by a particle system. They can be used for a countless number of impressive visual effects. Godot's particle system is quite powerful; too powerful to fully explore here, but you'll learn enough to get started experimenting with it.

- **Player shield:** If you're finding the game too hard, especially on higher levels where there are a lot of rocks, adding a shield to the player will greatly increase your chances of survival. You can also make larger rocks do more damage to the shield than smaller ones. You'll also make a nice display bar on the HUD to show the player's remaining shield level.

Sound/music

In the res://assets/sounds folder are several audio files containing different sounds in the **OggVorbis** format. By default, Godot sets .ogg files to loop when imported. In the case of explosion.ogg, laser_blast.ogg, and levelup.ogg, you don't want the sounds to loop, so you need to change the import settings for those files. To do this, select the file in the **FileSystem** dock, and then click the **Import** tab located next to the **Scene** tab on the right-hand side of the editor window. Uncheck the box next to **Loop** and click **Reimport**. Do this for each of the three sounds. Refer to the following screenshot:

To play a sound, it needs to be loaded by an `AudioStreamPlayer` node. Add two of these nodes to the `Player` scene, naming them `LaserSound` and `EngineSound`. Drag the respective sound into each node's **Stream** property in the **Inspector**. To play the sound when shooting, add the following line to `shoot()` in `Player.gd`:

```
$LaserSound.play()
```

Play the game and try shooting. If you find the sound a bit too loud, you can adjust the **Volume Db** property. Try a value of `-10`.

The engine sound works a little differently. It needs to play when the thrust is on, but if you try to just `play()` the sound in the `get_input()` function, it will restart the sound every frame as long as you have the input pressed. This doesn't sound good, so you only want to start playing the sound if it isn't already playing. Here is the relevant section from the `get_input()` function:

```
if Input.is_action_pressed("thrust"):
    thrust = Vector2(engine_power, 0)
    if not $EngineSound.playing:
        $EngineSound.play()
else:
    $EngineSound.stop()
```

Note that a problem can occur—if the player dies while holding down the thrust key, the engine sound will remain stuck on. This can be solved by adding `$EngineSound.stop()` to the `DEAD` state in `change_state()`.

In the `Main` scene, add three more `AudioStreamPlayer` nodes: `ExplodeSound`, `LevelupSound`, and `Music`. In their **Stream** properties, drop `explosion.ogg`, `levelup.ogg`, and `Funky-Gameplay_Looping.ogg`.

Add `$ExplodeSound.play()` as the first line of `_on_Rock_exploded()`, and add `$LevelupSound.play()` to `new_level()`.

To start/stop the music, add `$Music.play()` to `new_game()` and `$Music.stop()` to `game_over()`.

The Enemy also needs an `ExplodeSound` and a `ShootSound`. You can use the same explosion as the player, but there is an `enemy_laser.wav` sound to use for the shot.

Particles

The player ship's thrust is a perfect use for particles, creating a streaming flame from the engine. Add a `Particles2D` node to the `Player` scene and name it `Exhaust`. You might want to zoom in on the ship image while you're doing this part.

When first created, the `Particles2D` node has a warning: *A material to process the particles is not assigned*. Particles will not be emitted until you assign a `Process Material` in the Inspector. Two types of materials are possible: `ShaderMaterial` and `ParticlesMaterial`. `ShaderMaterial` allows you to write shader code in a GLSL-like language, while `ParticlesMaterial` is configured in the **Inspector**. Next to **Particles Material**, click the down-arrow and choose **New ParticlesMaterial**.

You'll see a line of white dots streaming down from the center of the player ship. Your challenge now is to turn those into an exhaust flame.

There are a very large number of properties to choose from when configuring particles, especially under `ParticlesMaterial`. Before starting on that, set these properties of the `Particles2D`:

- **Amount**: 25
- **Transform/Position**: (-28, 0)
- **Transform/Rotation**: 180
- **Visibility/Show Behind Parent**: On

Now, click on the `ParticlesMaterial`. This is where you'll find the majority of the properties that affect the particles' behavior. Start with **Emission Shape**—change it to **Box**. This will reveal **Box Extents**, which should be set to (1, 5, 1). Now, the particles are emitted over a small area instead of a single point.

Next, set **Spread/Spread** to 0 and **Gravity/Gravity** to (0, 0, 0). Now, the particles aren't falling or spreading out, but they are moving very slowly.

The next property is **Initial Velocity**. Set **Velocity** to 400. Then, scroll down to **Scale** and set it to 8.

To make the size change over time, you can set a **Scale Curve**. Click on **New CurveTexture** and click on it. A new panel labeled **Curve** will appear. The left-hand dot represents the starting scale, and the right-hand dot represents the end. Drag the right-hand dot down until your curve looks something like this:

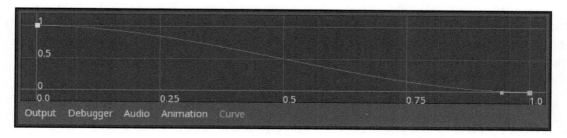

Now, the particles are shrinking as they age. Click the left arrow at the top of the **Inspector** to go back to the previous section.

The final section to adjust is **Color**. To make the particles appear like a flame, the particles should start out a bright orange-yellow and shift to red while fading out. In the **Color Ramp** property, click on **New GradientTexture**. Then, in the **Gradient** property, choose **New Gradient**:

The sliders labeled **1** and **2** select the starting and ending colors, while **3** shows what color is set on the currently selected slider. Click on slider **1** and then click **3** to choose an orange color, then click on slider **2** and set it to a deep red.

Now that we can see what the particles are doing, they are lasting far too long. Go back to the `Exhaust` node and change the **Lifetime** to `0.1`.

Hopefully, your ship's exhaust looks somewhat like a flame. If it doesn't, feel free to adjust the `ParticlesMaterial` properties until you are happy with it.

Now that the ship's `Exhaust` is configured, it needs to be turned on/off based on the player input. Go to the player script and add `$Exhaust.emitting = false` at the beginning of `get_input()`. Then, add `$Exhaust.emitting = true` under the `if` statement that checks for thrust input.

Enemy trail

You can also use particles to make a trail effect behind the enemy. Add a `Particles2D` to the enemy scene and set the properties as follows:

- **Amount**: `20`
- **Local Coords**: `Off`
- **Texture**: `res://assets/corona.png`
- **Show Behind Parent**: `On`

Note that the effect texture you're using is white on a black background. This image needs its blend mode changed. To do this, on the particle node, find the **Material** property (it is in the `CanvasItem` section). Select **New CanvasItemMaterial** and, in the resulting material, change the **Blend Mode** to `Add`.

Now, create a `ParticlesMaterial` like you did previously, and use these settings:

- **Emission Shape**:
    - **Shape**: **Box**
    - **Box Extents**: (25, 25, 1)
- **Spread**: `25`
- **Gravity**: (0, 0, 0)

Now, create a `ScaleCurve` like you did for the player exhaust. This time, make the curve look something like the following:

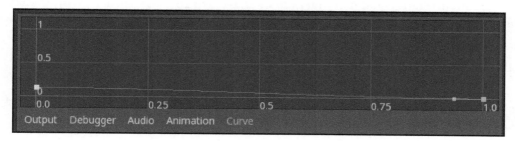

Try running the game and see how it looks. Feel free to tinker with the settings until you have something you like.

Player shield

In this section, you'll add a shield to the player and a display element to the HUD showing the current shield level.

First, add the following to the top of the `Player.gd` script:

```
signal shield_changed

export (int) var max_shield
export (float) var shield_regen

var shield = 0 setget set_shield
```

The `shield` variable will work similarly to `lives`, emitting a signal to the HUD whenever it changes. Save the script and set `max_shield` to `100` and `shield_regen` to `5` in the **Inspector**.

Next, add the following function, which handles changing the shield's value:

```
func set_shield(value):
    if value > max_shield:
        value = max_shield
    shield = value
    emit_signal("shield_changed", shield/max_shield)
    if shield <= 0:
        self.lives -= 1
```

Also, since some things, such as regeneration, may add to the shield's value, you need to make sure it doesn't go above the maximum allowed value. Then, when you send the shield_changed signal, you pass the ratio of shield/max_shield. This way, the HUD's display doesn't need to know anything about the actual values, just the shield's relative state.

Add this line to start() and to set_lives():

```
self.shield = max_shield
```

Hitting a rock will damage the shield, and bigger rocks should do more damage:

```
func _on_Player_body_entered( body ):
    if body.is_in_group('rocks'):
        body.explode()
        $Explosion.show()
        $Explosion/AnimationPlayer.play("explosion")
        self.shield -= body.size * 25
```

The enemy's bullets should also do damage, so make this change to EnemyBullet.gd:

```
func _on_EnemyBullet_body_entered(body):
    if body.name == 'Player':
        body.shield -= 15
    queue_free()
```

Also, running into the enemy should damage the player, so update this in Enemy.gd:

```
func _on_Enemy_body_entered(body):
    if body.name == 'Player':
        body.shield -= 50
        explode()
```

The last addition to the player script is to regenerate the shield each frame. Add this line to _process():

```
self.shield += shield_regen * delta
```

The next step is to add the display element to the HUD. Rather than display the shield's value in a Label, you'll use a TextureProgress node. This is a Control node that is a type of ProgressBar: a node that displays a given value as a filled bar. The TextureProgress node allows you to assign a texture to be used for the bar's display.

In the existing `HBoxContainer`, add `TextureRect` and `TextureProgress`. Place them after the `ScoreLabel` and before the `LivesCounter`. Change the name of the `TextureProgress` to **ShieldBar**. Your node setup should look like this:

Drag the `res://assets/shield_gold.png` texture into the *Texture* property of `TextureRect`. This will be an icon indicating what the bar is displaying.

The **ShieldBar** has three texture properties: Under, Over, and Progress. Progress is the texture that will be displayed as the bar's value. Drag `res://assets/barHorizontal_green_mid 200.png` into this property. The other two texture properties allow you to customize the appearance by setting an image to be drawn below or above the progress texture. Drag `res://assets/glassPanel_200.png` into the *Over* texture property.

In the *Range* section, you can set the numeric properties of the bar. **Min Value** and **Max Value** should be set to 0 and 100, as this bar will be showing the percentage value of the shield, not its raw value. Value is the property that controls the currently displayed fill value. Change it to 75 to see the bar partly filled. Also, set its **Horizontal** size flags to **Fill, Expand**.

Now, you can update the HUD script to control the shield bar. Add these variables at the top:

```
onready var ShieldBar = $MarginContainer/HBoxContainer/ShieldBar
var red_bar = preload("res://assets/barHorizontal_red_mid 200.png")
var green_bar = preload("res://assets/barHorizontal_green_mid 200.png")
var yellow_bar = preload("res://assets/barHorizontal_yellow_mid 200.png")
```

In addition to the green bar texture, you also have red and yellow bars in the `assets` folder. This will allow you to change the shield's color as the value decreases. Loading the textures in this way makes them easier to access later in the script when you want to assign the appropriate image to the `TextureProgress` node:

```
func update_shield(value):
    ShieldBar.texture_progress = green_bar
    if value < 40:
        ShieldBar.texture_progress = red_bar
    elif value < 70:
        ShieldBar.texture_progress = yellow_bar
    ShieldBar.value = value
```

Lastly, click on the `Main` scene's `Player` node and connect the `shield_changed` signal to the `update_shield()` function you just created. Run the game and verify that you can see the shield and that it is working. You may want to increase or decrease the regeneration rate to adjust it to a speed you like.

Summary

In this chapter, you learned how to work with `RigidBody2D` nodes and learned more about how Godot's physics works. You also implemented a basic Finite State Machine—something you'll find more and more useful as your projects grow larger. You saw how `Container` nodes help organize and keep UI nodes aligned. Finally, you added some sound effects and got your first taste of advanced visual effects by using the `AnimationPlayer` and `Particles2D` nodes.

You also created a number of game objects using the standard Godot hierarchies, such as `CollisionShapes` being attached to `CollisionObjects`. At this point, some of these node configurations should be starting to look familiar to you.

Before moving on, look through the project again. Play it. Make sure you understand what each scene is doing, and read through the scripts to review how everything connects together.

In the next chapter, you'll learn about kinematic bodies, and use them to create a side-scrolling platform game.

5
Jungle Jump (Platformer)

In this chapter, you'll build a classic *platform*, style game in the tradition of *Super Mario Bros.* Platform games are a very popular genre, and understanding how they work can help you make a variety of different game styles. The physics of platformers can be deceptively complex, and you'll see how Godot's `KinematicBody2D` physics node has features to help you implement the character controller features you need for a satisfying experience. Take a look at the following screenshot:

In this project, you will learn about:

- Using the `KinematicBody2D` physics node
- Combining animations and user input to produce complex character behavior
- Creating an infinitely scrolling background using ParallaxLayers
- Organizing your project and planning for expansion

Project setup

Create a new project. Before you download the assets from the link that follows, you need to prepare the import settings for the game art. The art assets for this project use a *pixel art* style, which means they look best when not filtered, which is Godot's default setting for textures. **Filtering** is a method by which the pixels of an image are smoothed. It can improve the look of some art, but not pixel-based images:

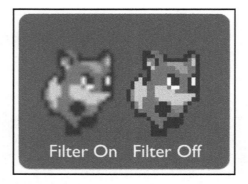

It's inconvenient to have to disable this for every image, so Godot allows you to customize the default import settings. Click on the `icon.png` file in the **FileSystem** dock, then click the **Import** tab next to the **Scene** tab on the right. This window allows you to change the import settings for the file you've selected. Uncheck the **Filter** property, then click **Preset** and choose **Set as Default for 'Texture'**. This way, all images will be imported with filtering disabled. Refer to the following screenshot:

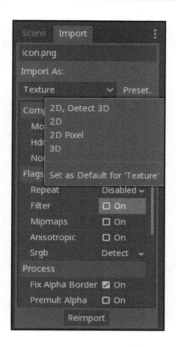

If you've already imported images, their import settings won't be updated automatically. After changing the default, you'll have to reimport any existing images. You can select multiple files in the **FileSystem** dock and click the **Reimport** button to apply the settings to many files at once.

Now, you can download the game assets from the following link and unzip them in your project folder. Godot will import all the images with the new default settings, `https://github.com/PacktPublishing/Godot-Game-Engine-Projects/releases`

Next, open **Project** | **Project Settings** and under **Rendering/Quality**, set **Use Pixel Snap** to `On`. This will ensure that all images will be aligned properly—something that will be very important when you're designing your game's levels.

While you have the settings window open, go to the **Display/Window** section and change **Stretch/Mode** to `2d` and **Aspect** to `expand`. These settings will allow the user to resize the game window while preserving the image's quality. Once the project has been completed, you'll be able to see the effects of this setting.

Next, set up the collision layer names so that it will be more convenient to set up collisions between different types of objects. Go to **Layer Names/2d Physics** and name the first four layers like this:

Finally, add the following actions for the player controls in the **Input Map** tab under **Project | Project Settings**:

Action Name	Key(s)
right	D, →
left	A, ←
jump	Space
crouch	S, ↓
climb	W, ↑

Introducing kinematic bodies

A platform game requires gravity, collisions, jumping, and other physics behavior, so you might think that RigidBody2D would be the perfect choice to implement the character's movement. In practice, however, you'll find that the *realistic* physics of the rigid body are not desirable for a platform character. To the player, realism is less important than responsive control and an *action* feel. As the developer, you therefore want to have precise control over the character's movements and collision response. For this reason, a kinematic body is usually the better choice for a platform character.

The KinematicBody2D node is designed for implementing bodies that are to be controlled directly by the user or via code. These nodes detect collisions with other bodies when moving, but are not affected by global physics properties like gravity or friction. This doesn't mean that a kinematic body can't be affected by gravity and other forces, just that you must calculate those forces and their effects in code; the engine will not move a kinematic body automatically.

When moving KinematicBody2D, as with RigidBody2D, you should not set its position directly. Instead, you use either the move_and_collide() or move_and_slide() methods. These methods move the body along a given vector and instantly stop if a collision is detected with another body. After KinematicBody2D has collided, any *collision response* must be coded manually.

Collision response

After a collision, you may want the body to bounce, to slide along a wall, or to alter the properties of the object it hit. The way you handle collision response depends on which method you used to move the body.

move_and_collide

When using move_and_collide(), the function returns a KinematicCollision2D object upon collision. This object contains information about the collision and the colliding body. You can use this information to determine the response. Note that the function returns null when the movement was completed successfully with no collision.

For example, if you want the body to bounce off of the colliding object, you could use the following script:

```
extends KinematicBody2D

var velocity = Vector2(250, 250)

func _physics_process(delta):
    var collide = move_and_collide(velocity * delta)
    if collide:
        velocity = velocity.bounce(collide.normal)
```

move_and_slide

Sliding is a very common option for collision response. Imagine a player moving along walls in a top-down game or running up and down slopes in a platformer. While it's possible to code this response yourself after using `move_and_collide()`, `move_and_slide()` provides a convenient way to implement sliding movement. When using this method, the body will automatically slide along the colliding surface. In addition, sliding collisions allow you to use methods like `is_on_floor()` to detect the orientation of the colliding surface.

Since this project will require not just moving along the ground, but also running up and down slopes, `move_and_slide()` is going to play a large role in your player's movement. You'll see how it works as you build up the player object.

Player scene

Open a new scene and add a `KinematicBody2D` object named `Player` as the root and save the scene (don't forget to click the **Make children unselectable** button). When saving the `Player` scene, you should also create a new folder to contain it. This will help keep your project folder organized as you add more scenes and scripts.

As you've done in other projects, you'll include all the nodes that the player character needs to function in the `Player` scene. For this game, that means handling collisions with various game objects, including platforms, enemies, and collectibles; displaying animations for actions, such as running or jumping; and a camera to follow the player around the level.

Scripting the various animations can quickly become unmanageable, so you'll use a *finite state machine* to manage and track the player's state. See `Chapter 3`, *Escape the Maze*, to review how the simplified FSM was built. You'll follow a similar pattern for this project.

Collision Layer/Mask

A body's collision layer property sets what layer(s) the body is found on. `Player` needs to be assigned to the player layer you named in **Project Settings**.

The **Collision/Mask** property allows you to set what types of objects the body will detect. Set the **Player** layer to `player` and its mask to **environment, enemies,** and **collectibles** (1, 3, and 4):

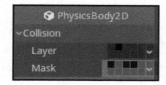

Sprite

Add a Sprite node to `Player`. Drag the `res://assets/player_sheet.png` file from the **FileSystem** dock and drop it in the **Texture** property of the `Sprite`. The player animation is saved in the form of a sprite sheet:

You'll use `AnimationPlayer` to handle the animations, so in the **Animation** properties of `Sprite`, set **Vframes** to 1 and **Hframes** to 19. Set **Frame** to 7 to begin, as this is the frame that shows the character standing still (it's the first frame of the `idle` animation):

Collision shape

As with other physics bodies, `KinematicBody2D` needs a shape assigned to define its collision bounds. Add a `CollisionShape2D` object and create a new `RectangleShape2D` object inside it. When sizing the rectangle, you want it to reach the bottom of the image but not be quite as wide. In general, making the collision shape a bit smaller than the image will result in a better *feel* when playing, avoiding the experience of hitting something that looks like it wouldn't result in a collision.

You'll also need to offset the shape a small amount to make it fit. Setting **Position** to (0, 5) works well. When you're done, it should look approximately like this:

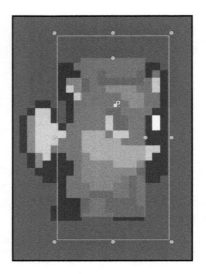

Shapes

Some developers prefer a capsule shape over a rectangle shape for sidescrolling characters. A capsule is a pill-shaped collision that's rounded on both ends:

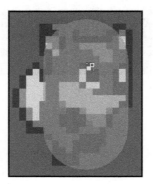

However, while this shape might seem to *cover* the sprite better, it can lead to difficulties when implementing platformer-style movement. For example, when standing too near the edge of a platform, the character may slide off due to the rounded bottom, which can be very frustrating for the player.

In some cases, depending on the complexity of your character and its interactions with other objects, you may want to add multiple shapes to the same object. You might have one shape at the character's feet to detect ground collisions, another on its body to detect damage (sometimes called a hurtbox), and yet another covering the player's front to detect contact with walls.

It's recommended that you stick to `RectangleShape2D`, as shown in the preceding screenshot, for this character. However, once you've finished the project, you should try changing the player's collision shape to `CapsuleShape2D` and observing the resulting behavior. If you like it better, feel free to use it instead.

Animations

Add an `AnimationPlayer` node to the `Player` scene. You'll use this node to change the **Frame** property on `Sprite` to display the character's animations. Start by making a new animation named `idle`:

Set **Length** to 0.4 seconds and keep **Step** at 0.1 seconds. Change the **Frame** of `Sprite` to 7 and click the **Add keyframe** button next to the **Frame** property to create a new animation track, then press it again, noting that it automatically increments the **Frame** property:

Continue pressing it until you have frames 7 through 10. Finally, click the **Enable/Disable looping** button to enable looping and then press **Play** to view your animation. Your animation setup should look like this:

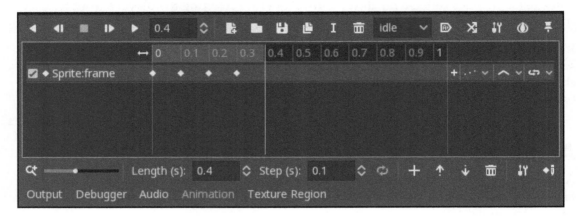

Now you need to repeat the process for the other animations. See the following table for a list of settings:

name	length	frames	looping
idle	0.4	7, 8, 9 ,10	on
run	0.5	13, 14, 15, 16, 17, 18	on
hurt	0.2	5, 6	on
jump_up	0.1	11	off
jump_down	0.1	12	Off

Finishing up the scene tree

Add Camera2D to the Player scene. This node will keep the game window centered on the player as it moves around the level. You can also use it to zoom in on the player, since the pixel art is relatively small. Remember, since you set filtering off in the import settings, the player's texture will remain pixelated and blocky when zoomed in.

To enable the camera, click the **Current** property to On, then set the **Zoom** property to (0.4, 0.4). Values smaller than one zoom the camera in, while larger values zoom it out.

Player states

The player character has a wide variety of behaviors, such as jumping, running, and crouching. Coding such behaviors can become very complex and hard to manage. One solution is to use Boolean variables (is_jumping or is_running, for example), but this leads to possibly confusing states (what if is_crouching and is_jumping are both true?) and quickly leads to spaghetti code.

A better solution to this problem is to use a state machine to handle the player's current state and control the transitions to other states. Finite state machines were discussed in Chapter 3, *Escape the Maze*.

Here is a diagram of the player's states and the transitions between them:

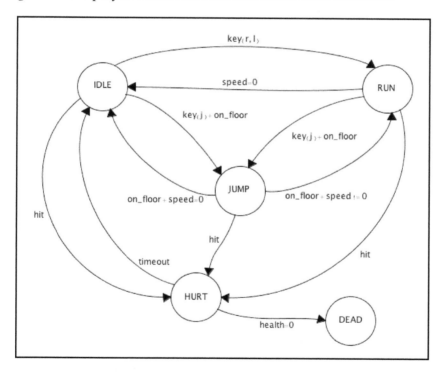

As you can see, state machine diagrams can become quite complex, even with a relatively small number of states.

Note that while the spritesheet contains animations for them, the CROUCH and CLIMB animations are not included here. This is to keep the number of states manageable at the beginning of the project. Later, you'll have the opportunity to add them to the player's state machine.

Player script

Attach a new script to the `Player` node. Add the following code to create the player's state machine:

```
extends KinematicBody2D
enum {IDLE, RUN, JUMP, HURT, DEAD}
var state
var anim
var new_anim

func ready():
    change_state(IDLE)

func change_state(new_state):
    state = new_state
    match state:
        IDLE:
            new_anim = 'idle'
        RUN:
            new_anim = 'run'
        HURT:
            new_anim = 'hurt'
        JUMP:
            new_anim = 'jump_up'
        DEAD:
            hide()

func _physics_process(delta):
    if new_anim != anim:
        anim = new_anim
        $AnimationPlayer.play(anim)
```

Once again, you're using `enum` to list the allowed states for the system. When you want to change the player's state, you'll call `change_state()`, for example: `change_state(IDLE)`. For now, the script only changes the animation value, but you'll add more state functionality later.

You may be asking, *why not just play the animation when the state changes? Why this new_anim business?* This is because when you call `play()` on `AnimationPlayer`, it starts the animation from the beginning. If you did that while running, for example, you'd only see the first frame of the run animation as it restarted every frame. By using the `new_anim` variable, you can let the current animation continue to play smoothly until you want it to change.

Player movement

The player needs three controls—left, right, and jump. The combination of the current state plus which keys are pressed will trigger a state change if the transition is allowed by the state rules. Add the `get_input()` function to process the inputs and determine the result:

```
extends KinematicBody2D

export (int) var run_speed
export (int) var jump_speed
export (int) var gravity

enum {IDLE, RUN, JUMP, HURT, DEAD}
var state
var anim
var new_anim
var velocity = Vector2()

func get_input():
    if state == HURT:
        return # don't allow movement during hurt state
    var right = Input.is_action_pressed('right')
    var left = Input.is_action_pressed('left')
    var jump = Input.is_action_just_pressed('jump')

    # movement occurs in all states
    velocity.x = 0
    if right:
        velocity.x += run_speed
        $Sprite.flip_h = false
    if left:
        velocity.x -= run_speed
        $Sprite.flip_h = true
    # only allow jumping when on the ground
    if jump and is_on_floor():
        change_state(JUMP)
        velocity.y = jump_speed
```

```
# IDLE transitions to RUN when moving
if state == IDLE and velocity.x != 0:
    change_state(RUN)
# RUN transitions to IDLE when standing still
if state == RUN and velocity.x == 0:
    change_state(IDLE)
# transition to JUMP when falling off an edge
if state in [IDLE, RUN] and !is_on_floor():
    change_state(JUMP)
```

Note that the jump check is using `is_action_just_pressed()` rather than `is_action_pressed()`. While the latter always returns `true` as long as the key is held down, the former is only `true` in the frame after the key was pressed. This means that the player must press the jump key each time they want to jump.

Now, call this function from `_physics_process()`, add the pull of gravity to the player's `velocity`, and call the `move_and_slide()` method to move the body:

```
func _physics_process(delta):
    velocity.y += gravity * delta
    get_input()
    if new_anim != anim:
        anim = new_anim
        $AnimationPlayer.play(anim)
    # move the player
    velocity = move_and_slide(velocity, Vector2(0, -1))
```

The second parameter of `move_and_slide()` is a *normal* vector, indicating what surface direction the engine should consider to be the ground. In physics and geometry, a *normal* is a vector perpendicular to a surface, defining the direction a surface is facing. Using `(0, -1)`, which is a vector pointing upwards, the top of a horizontal surface will be considered as ground. Refer to the following screenshot:

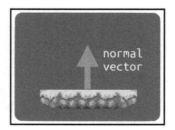

After moving with `move_and_slide()`, the physics engine will use this information to set the value of the `is_on_floor()`, `is_on_wall()` and `is_on_ceiling` methods. You can use this fact to detect when the jump ends by adding this after the move:

```
if state == JUMP and is_on_floor():
    change_state(IDLE)
```

Finally, the jump will look better if the animation switches from `jump_up` to `jump_down` when falling:

```
if state == JUMP and velocity.y > 0:          new_anim =
'jump_down'Testing the moves
```

At this point, it would be a good idea to test out the movement and make sure everything is working. You can't just run the player scene though, because the player will just start falling without a surface to stand on.

Create a new scene and add a `Node` called `Main` (later, this will become your real main scene). Add an instance of the `Player`, then add a `StaticBody2D` with a rectangular `CollisionShape2D`. Stretch the collision shape horizontally so that it's wide enough to walk back and forth on (like a platform) and place it below the character:

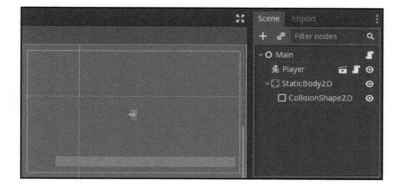

Press **Play Scene** and you should see the player stop falling and run the `idle` animation when it hits the static body.

Before moving on, make sure that all the movement and animations are working correctly. Run and jump in all directions and check that the correct animations are playing whenever the state changes. If you find any problems, review the previous sections and make sure you didn't miss a step.

Later, once the level is complete, the player will be passed a spawn location. To handle this, add this function to the `Player.gd` script:

```
func start(pos):
    position = pos
    show()
    change_state(IDLE)
```

Player health

Eventually, the player is going to encounter danger, so you should add a damage system. The player will start with three *hearts* and lose one each time they are damaged.

Add the following to the top of the script:

```
signal life_changed
signal dead

var life
```

The `life_changed` signal will be emitted whenever the value of `life` changes, notifying the display to update. `dead` will be emitted when `life` reaches 0. Add these two lines to the `start()` function:

```
life = 3
emit_signal('life_changed', life)
```

There are two possible ways for the player to be hurt: running into a *spike* object in the environment, or being hit by an enemy. In either event, the following function can be called:

```
func hurt():
    if state != HURT:
        change_state(HURT)
```

This is being nice to the player: if they're already hurt, they can't get hurt again (at least for the brief time until the *hurt* animation has stopped playing).

There are several things to do when the state changes to HURT in `change_state()`:

```
HURT:
    new_anim = 'hurt'
    velocity.y = -200
    velocity.x = -100 * sign(velocity.x)
    life -= 1
```

```
    emit_signal('life_changed', life)
    yield(get_tree().create_timer(0.5), 'timeout')
    change_state(IDLE)
    if life <= 0:
        change_state(DEAD)
DEAD:
    emit_signal('dead')
    hide()
```

Not only does does the player lose a life, but they are also bounced up and away from the damaging object. After a short time, the state changes back to IDLE.

Also, input will be disabled while the player is in the HURT state. Add this to the beginning of get_input():

```
if state == HURT:
    return
```

Now, the player is ready to take damage once the rest of the game is set up.

Collectible items

Before you start making the level, you need to create some pickups for the player to collect, since those will be part of the level as well. The assets/sprites folder contains sprite sheets for two types of collectibles: cherries and gems.

Rather than make separate scenes for each type of item, you can use a single scene and merely swap out the sprite sheet texture. Both objects will have the same behavior: animating in place and disappearing (that is, being collected) when contacted by the player. You can also add a Tween animation for the pickup (see Chapter 1, *Introduction*, for an example).

Collectible scene

Start the new scene with an Area2D and name it Collectible. An area is a good choice for these objects because you want to detect when the player contacts them (using the body_entered signal), but you don't need collision response from them. In the **Inspector**, set the **Collision/Layer** to **collectibles** (layer 4) and the **Collision/Mask** to **player** (layer 2). This will ensure that only the Player node will be able to collect an item while the enemies will pass right through.

Add three child nodes: `Sprite`, `CollisionShape2D`, and `AnimationPlayer`, then drag the `res://assets/cherry.png` Sprite sheet into the Sprite's **Texture**. Set the **Vframes** to 1 and **Hframes** to 5. Add a rectangle shape to `CollisionShape2D` and size it appropriately.

 As a general rule, you should size your objects' collision shapes so that they benefit the player. This means that enemy hitboxes should generally be a little smaller than the image while the hitboxes of beneficial items should be slightly oversized. This reduces player frustration and results in a better gameplay experience.

Add a new animation to `AnimationPlayer` (you only need one, so you can just name it `anim`). Set the **Length** to `1.6` seconds and the **Step** to `0.2` seconds.

Set the Sprite's **Frame** property to `0` and click the keyframe button to create the track. When you reach frame number four, start reversing the order back down to `1`. The full sequence of keyframes should be:

$$0 \rightarrow 1 \rightarrow 2 \rightarrow 3 \rightarrow 4 \rightarrow 3 \rightarrow 2 \rightarrow 1$$

Enable looping and press the **Play** button. Now, you have a nicely animated cherry! Drag `res://assets/gem.png` into the texture and check that it animates as well. Finally, click the **Autoplay on Load** button to ensure the animation will play automatically when the scene begins. Refer to the following screenshot:

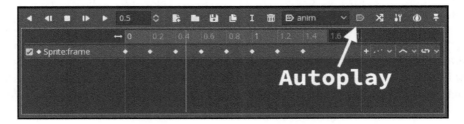

Collectible script

The Collectible's script needs to do two things:

- Set the start conditions (`texture` and `position`)
- Detect when the player enters the area

For the first part, add the following code to the new script:

```
extends Area2D

signal pickup

var textures = {'cherry': 'res://assets/sprites/cherry.png',
                'gem': 'res://assets/sprites/gem.png'}

func init(type, pos):
    $Sprite.texture = load(textures[type])
    position = pos
```

The `pickup` signal will be emitted when the player collects the item. In the `textures` dictionary, you have a list of the item types and their corresponding texture locations. Note that you can quickly paste those file paths by right-clicking on the file in the **FileSystem** dock and choosing **Copy Path**:

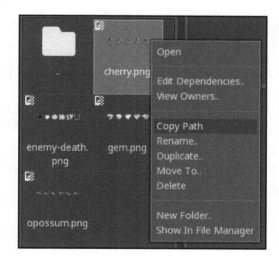

Next, you have an `init()` function that sets the `texture` and `position` to the given values. The level script will use this function to spawn all the collectibles that you add to your level map.

Finally, you need the object to detect when it's been picked up. Click on the `Area2D` and connect its `body_entered` signal. Add the following code to the created function:

```
func _on_Collectible_body_entered(body):
    emit_signal('pickup')
    queue_free()
```

Emitting the signal will allow the game's script to react appropriately to the item pickup. It can add to the score, increase the player's speed, or whatever other effect you want the item to apply.

Designing the level

It wouldn't be a platformer without jumps. For most readers, this section will take up the largest chunk of time. Once you start designing a level, you'll find it's a lot of fun to lay out all the pieces, creating challenging jumps, secret paths, and dangerous encounters.

First, you'll create a generic `Level` scene containing all the nodes and code that is common to all levels. You can then create any number of level scenes that inherit from this master level.

TileSet configuration

In the `assets` folder you downloaded at the beginning of the project is a `tilesets` folder. It contains three ready-made `TileSet` resources using the 16x16 art for the game:

- `tiles_world.tres`: Ground and platform tiles
- `tiles_items.tres`: Decorative items, foreground objects, and collectibles
- `tiles_spikes.tres`: Danger items

It is recommended that you use these tile sets to create the levels for this project. However, if you would rather make them yourself, the original art is in `res://assets/environment/layers`. See `Chapter 2`, *Coin Dash*, to review how to create a `TileSet` resource.

Base-level setup

Create a new scene and add a `Node2D` named `Level`. Save the scene in a new folder called `levels`. This is where you'll save any other levels you create, after inheriting from `Level.tscn`. The node hierarchy will be the same for all levels—only the layout will be different.

Next, add a `TileMap` and set its **Cell/Size** to `(16, 16)`, then duplicate it three times (press *Ctrl + D* to duplicate a node). These will be the layers of your level, holding different tiles and information about the layout. Name the four `TileMap` instances as follows and drag-and-drop the corresponding `TileSet` into the **Tile Set** property of each. Refer to the following table:

TileMap	Tile Set
World	tiles_world.tres
Objects	tiles_items.tres
Pickups	tiles_items.tres
Danger	tiles_spikes.tres

 It's a good idea to press the Lock button on your `TileMap` nodes to prevent accidentally moving them while you're working on your map.

Next, add an instance of the `Player` scene and a `Position2D` named `PlayerSpawn`. Click the hide button on the `Player`—you'll use `show()` in the level script to make the player appear when it starts. Your scene tree should now look like this:

Attach a script to the `Level` node:

```
extends Node2D

onready var pickups = $Pickups

func _ready():
    pickups.hide()
    $Player.start($PlayerSpawn.position)
```

Later, you'll be scanning the `Pickups` map to spawn collectible items in the designated locations. This map layer itself shouldn't be seen, but rather than set it as hidden in the scene tree, which is easy to forget before you run the game, you can make sure it's always hidden during gameplay by doing so in `_ready()`. Because there will be many references to the node, storing the result of `$Pickups` in the `pickups` variable will cache the result. (Remember, `$NodeName` is the same as writing `get_node("NodeName")`.)

Designing the first level

Now, you're ready to start drawing the level! Click **Scene | New Inherited Scene** and choose `Level.tscn`. Name the new node `Level01` and save it (still in the `levels` folder).

Start with the `World` map and be creative. Do you like lots of jumps, or twisty tunnels to explore? Long runs, or careful upward climbs?

Before going too far in your design, experiment with jump distance. You can change the Player's `jump_speed`, `run_speed`, and `gravity` properties to alter how high and how far they can jump. Set up some different gap sizes and run the scene to try them out. Don't forget to drag the `PlayerSpawn` node to the place you want the character to start.

For example, can the player make this jump? Take a look at the following screenshot:

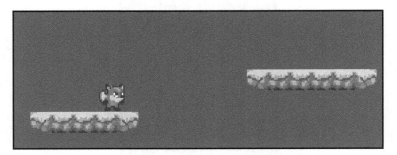

How you set the player's movement properties will have a big impact on how your level should be laid out. Make sure you're happy with your settings before spending too much time on the full design.

Once you have the `World` layer set up, use the `Objects` layer to place decorations and accents like plants, rocks, and vines.

Use the `Pickups` layer to mark the locations you'll spawn collectible items at. There are two kinds: gems and cherries. The tiles that spawn them are drawn with a magenta background to make them stand out. Remember, they'll be replaced at runtime by the actual items and the tiles themselves won't be seen.

Once you have your level laid out, you can limit the horizontal scrolling of the player camera to match the size of the map (plus a 5 tile buffer on each end):

```
signal score_changed
var score

func _ready():
    score = 0
    emit_signal('score_changed', score)
    pickups.hide()
    $Player.start($PlayerSpawn.position)
    set_camera_limits()

func set_camera_limits():
    var map_size = $World.get_used_rect()
    var cell_size = $World.cell_size
    $Player/Camera2D.limit_left = (map_size.position.x - 5) * cell_size.x
    $Player/Camera2D.limit_right = (map_size.end.x + 5) * cell_size.x
```

The script also needs to scan the `Pickups` layer and look for the item markers:

```
func spawn_pickups():
    for cell in pickups.get_used_cells():
        var id = pickups.get_cellv(cell)
        var type = pickups.tile_set.tile_get_name(id)
        if type in ['gem', 'cherry']:
            var c = Collectible.instance()
            var pos = pickups.map_to_world(cell)
            c.init(type, pos + pickups.cell_size/2)
            add_child(c)
            c.connect('pickup', self, '_on_Collectible_pickup')

func _on_Collectible_pickup():
    score += 1
    emit_signal('score_changed', score)

func _on_Player_dead():
    pass
```

This function uses `get_used_cells()` to get an array of the tiles that are in use on the `Pickups` map. The `TileMap` sets each tile's value to an `id` that references the individual tile object in the `TileSet`. You can then query the `TileSet` for the tile's name using `tile_set.tile_get_name()`.

Add `spawn_pickups()` to `_ready()` and add the following at the top of the script:

```
var Collectible = preload('res://items/Collectible.tscn')
```

Try running your level and you should see your gems and/or cherries appear where you placed them. Also check that they disappear when you run into them.

Scrolling background

There are two background images in the `res://assets/environment/layers` folder: `back.png` and `middle.png`, for the far and near background, respectively. By placing these images behind the tilemap and scrolling them at different speeds relative to the camera, you can create an attractive illusion of depth in the background.

To start, add a `ParallaxBackground` node to the `Level` scene. This node works automatically along with the camera to create a scrolling effect. Drag this node to the top of the scene tree so that it will be drawn behind the rest of the nodes. Next, add a `ParallaxLayer` node as a child—`ParallaxBackground` can have any number of `ParallaxLayer` as children, allowing you to make many independently scrolling layers. Add a `Sprite` node as a child to the `ParallaxLayer` and drag the `res://assets/environment/layers/back.png` image into the **Texture**. Important—uncheck the box next to the **Centered** property of the **Sprite**.

The background image is a little small, so set the Sprite's **Scale** to `(1.5, 1.5)`.

On the `ParallaxLayer`, set the **Motion/Scale** to `(0.2, 1)`. This setting controls how fast the background scrolls in relation to the camera. By setting it to a low number, the background will only move a small amount as the player moves left and right.

Next, you want to be sure the image repeats if your level is very wide, so set **Mirroring** to `(576, 0)`. This is exactly the width of the image (`384` times `1.5`), so the image will be repeated when it has moved by that amount.

Note that this background is best for wide rather than tall levels. If you jump too high, you'll reach the top of the background image and suddenly see the grey emptiness again. You can fix this by setting the top limit of the camera. If you haven't moved it, the upper-left corner of the image will be at `(0, 0)`, so you can set the **Top** limit on the camera to `0`. If you've moved the `ParallaxLayer`, you can find the correct value by looking at the `y` value of the node's **Position**.

Now, add another `ParallaxLayer` (as a sibling of the first) for the middle background layer and give it a `Sprite` child. This time, use the `res://assets/environment/layers/middle.png` texture. This texture is much narrower than the cloud/sky image, so you'll need to do a little extra adjustment to make it repeat properly. This is because the `ParallaxBackground` needs to have images that are at least as big as the viewport area.

First, click on the texture in the **FileSystem** dock and select the **Import** tab. Change the **Repeat** property to **Mirrored**, and check `On` for **Mipmaps**. Press **Reimport**. Now, the texture can be repeated to fill the screen (and the parallax system will repeat it after that):

The image's original size is `176x368`, and it needs to be repeated horizontally. In the `Sprite` properties, click **On** for **Region Enabled**. Next, set the **Rect** property to `(0, 0, 880, 368)` (880 is 176 times 5, so you should now see five repetitions of the image). Move the `ParallaxLayer` so that the image overlaps the bottom half of the ocean/cloud image:

Set the `ParallaxLayer` **Motion/Scale** to `(0.6, 1)` and the **Mirroring** to `(880, 0)`. Using a higher scale factor means this layer will scroll a little faster than the cloud layer behind it, giving a satisfying effect of depth, as shown in the following screenshot:

Once you're sure everything is working, try adjusting the **Scale** value for both layers and see how it changes. For example, try a value of `(1.2, 1)` on the middle layer for a much different visual effect.

Your main scene's tree should now look like this:

Dangerous objects

The **Danger** map layer is meant to hold the spike objects that will harm the player if they're touched. Try placing a few of them on your map where you can easily test running into them. Note that because of the way TileMaps work, colliding with *any* tile on this layer will cause damage to the player!

About slide collisions

When a `KinematicBody2D` is moved with `move_and_slide()`, it may collide with more than one object in a given frame. For example, when running into a corner, the character may hit the wall and the floor at the same time. You can use the `get_slide_count()` method to find out how many collisions occurred, and then get information about each collision with `get_slide_collision()`.

In the case of the `Player`, you want to detect when a collision occurs against the Danger `TileMap` object. You can do this just after using `move_and_slide()` in `Player.gd`:

```
velocity = move_and_slide(velocity, Vector2(0, -1))
if state == HURT:
    return
for idx in range(get_slide_count()):
    var collision = get_slide_collision(idx)
    if collision.collider.name == 'Danger':
        hurt()
```

Before checking for a collision with `Danger`, you can check whether the player is already in the `HURT` state and skip checking if it is. Next, you must use `get_slide_count()` to iterate through any collisions that may have occurred. For each, you can check whether the `collider.name` is `Danger`.

Run the scene and try running into one of the spike objects. Just like you wrote in the `hurt()` function previously, you should see the player change to the `HURT` state for a brief time before returning to `IDLE`. After three hits, the player enters the `DEAD` state, which currently sets the visibility to hidden.

Enemies

Currently, the map is very lonely, so it's time to add some enemies to liven things up.

There are many different behaviors you could create for an enemy. For this project, the enemy will walk along a platform in a straight line and reverse direction when hitting an obstacle.

Scene setup

Start with `KinematicBody2D` with three children: `Sprite`, `AnimationPlayer`, and `CollisionShape2D`. Save the scene as `Enemy.tscn` in a new folder called `enemies`. If you decide to add more enemy types to the game, you can save them all here.

Set the body's collision layer to `enemies` and its collision masks to `environment`, `player`, and `enemies`. It's also useful to group the enemies, so click on the **Node** tab and add the body to a group called `enemies`.

Add the `res://assets/opossum.png` sprite sheet to the Sprite's **Texture**. Set **Vframes** to 1 and **Hframes** to 6. Add a rectangular collision shape that covers most (but not all) of the image, making sure that the bottom of the collision shape is aligned with the bottom of the image's feet:

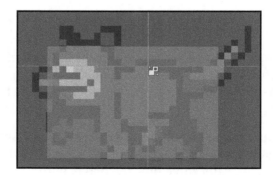

Add a new animation to the `AnimationPlayer` called `walk`. Set the **Length** to 0.6 seconds and the **Step** to 0.1 seconds. Turn on **Looping** and **Autoplay**.

The `walk` animation will have two tracks: one that sets the **Texture** property and one that changes the **Frame** property. Click the **Add keyframe** button next to **Texture** once to add the first track, then click the one next to **Frame** and repeat until you have frames 0 through 5. Press **Play** and verify that the walk animation is playing correctly. The **Animation** panel should look like this:

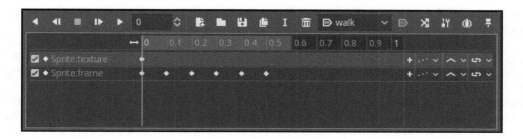

Script

Add the following script:

```
extends KinematicBody2D

export (int) var speed
export (int) var gravity

var velocity = Vector2()
var facing = 1

func _physics_process(delta):
    $Sprite.flip_h = velocity.x > 0
    velocity.y += gravity * delta
    velocity.x = facing * speed

    velocity = move_and_slide(velocity, Vector2(0, -1))
    for idx in range(get_slide_count()):
        var collision = get_slide_collision(idx)
        if collision.collider.name == 'Player':
            collision.collider.hurt()
        if collision.normal.x != 0:
            facing = sign(collision.normal.x)
            velocity.y = -100

    if position.y > 1000:
        queue_free()
```

In this script, the `facing` variable tracks the direction of movement (1 or −1). As with the player, when moving, you iterate through the slide collisions. If the colliding object is the `Player`, you call its `hurt()` function.

Next, you can check whether the colliding body's normal vector has an x component that isn't 0. This means it points to the left or right (that is, it is a wall, crate, or other obstacle). The direction of the *normal* is used to set the new facing. Finally, giving the body a small upward velocity will make the reverse transition look more appealing.

Lastly, if, for some reason, the enemy does fall off a platform, you don't want the game to have to track it falling forever, so delete any enemy whose y coordinate becomes too big.

Set **Speed** to 50 and **Gravity** to 900 in the **Inspector**, and then create an `Enemy` in your level scene. Make sure it has an obstacle on either side, and play the scene. Check that the enemy walks back and forth between the obstacles. Try putting the player in its path and verify that the player's `hurt()` method is getting called.

Damaging the enemy

It's not fair if the player can't strike back, so in the tradition of Super Mario Bros., jumping on top of the enemy will defeat it.

Start by adding a new animation to the `AnimationPlayer` of the `Enemy` and name it `death`. Set the **Length** to 0.3 seconds and the **Step** to 0.05. *Don't* turn on looping for this animation.

This animation will also set the **Texture** and **Frame**. This time, drag the `res://assets/enemy-death.png` image into the Sprite's **Texture** before adding the keyframe for that property. As before, keyframe all the `Frame` values from 0 through 5. Press Play to see the death animation run.

Add the following code to the Enemy's script:

```
func take_damage():
    $AnimationPlayer.play('death')
    $CollisionShape2D.disabled = true
    set_physics_process(false)
```

When the `Player` hits the `Enemy` under the right conditions, it will call `take_damage()`, which plays the `death` animation. It also disables collision and movement for the duration of the animation.

When the `death` animation finishes, it's OK to remove the enemy, so connect the `animation_finished()` signal of `AnimationPlayer`. This signal is called every time an animation finishes, so you need to check that it's the correct one:

```
func _on_AnimationPlayer_animation_finished(anim_name):
    if anim_name == 'death':
        queue_free()
```

To complete the process, go to the `Player.gd` script and add the following to the collision checks in the `_physics_process()` method:

```
for idx in range(get_slide_count()):
    var collision = get_slide_collision(idx)
    if collision.collider.name == 'Danger':
        hurt()
    if collision.collider.is_in_group('enemies'):
        var player_feet = (position + $CollisionShape2D.shape.extents).y
        if player_feet < collision.collider.position.y:
            collision.collider.take_damage()
            velocity.y = -200
        else:
            hurt()
```

This code checks the *y* coordinate of the player's feet (that is, the bottom of its collision shape) against the enemy's *y* coordinate. If the player is higher, the enemy is hurt; otherwise, the player is.

Run the level and try jumping on the enemy to make sure all is working as expected.

HUD

The purpose of the HUD is to display the information the player needs to know during gameplay. Collecting items will increase the player's score, so that information needs to be displayed. The player also needs to see their remaining life value, which will be displayed as a series of hearts.

Scene setup

Create a new scene with a `MarginContainer` node. Name it `HUD` and save in the `ui` folder. Set the **Layout** to **Top Wide**. In the **Custom Constants** section of **Inspector**, set the following values:

- **Margin Right**: 50
- **Margin Top**: 20
- **Margin Left**: 50
- **Margin Bottom**: 20

Add an `HBoxContainer`. This node will contain all the UI elements and keep them aligned. It will have two children:

- Label: ScoreLabel
- HBoxContainer: LifeCounter

On the `ScoreLabel`, set the **Text** property to 1, and under **Size Flags**, set **Horizontal** to **Fill** and **Expand**. Add a custom `DynamicFont` using `res://assets/Kenney Thick.ttf` from the `assets` folder, with a font size of 48. In the **Custom Colors** section, set the **Font Color** to `white` and the **Font Color Shadow** to `black`. Finally, under **Custom Constants**, set **Shadow Offset X**, **Shadow Offset Y**, and **Shadow As Outline** all to 5. You should see a large white **1** with a black outline.

For the `LifeCounter`, add a `TextureRect` and name it `L1`. Drag `res://assets/heart.png` into its **Texture** and set **Stretch Mode** to `Keep Aspect Centered`. Click on the node and press *Ctrl + D* four times so that you have a row of five hearts:

When finished, your HUD should look like this:

Script

Here is the script for the HUD:

```
extends MarginContainer

onready var life_counter = [$HBoxContainer/LifeCounter/L1,
                            $HBoxContainer/LifeCounter/L2,
                            $HBoxContainer/LifeCounter/L3,
                            $HBoxContainer/LifeCounter/L4,
                            $HBoxContainer/LifeCounter/L5]

func _on_Player_life_changed(value):
    for heart in range(life_counter.size()):
        life_counter[heart].visible = value > heart

func _on_score_changed(value):
    $HBoxContainer/ScoreLabel.text = str(value)
```

First, you make an array of references to the five heart indicators. Then, in
`_on_Player_life_changed()`, which will be called when the player gets hurt or healed,
you calculate how many hearts to display by setting `visible` to `false` if the number of the
heart is less than the life amount.

`_on_score_changed()` is similar, changing the value of the `ScoreLabel` when called.

Attaching the HUD

Open `Level.tscn` (the base-level scene, *not* your `Level01` scene) and add a `CanvasLayer`
node. Instance the HUD scene as a child of this `CanvasLayer`.

Click on the `Player` node and connect its `life_changed` signal to the HUD's `_on_Player_life_changed()` method:

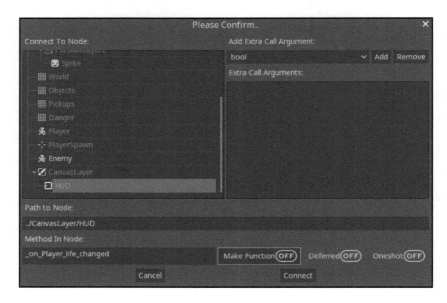

Next, do the same with the `score_changed` signal of the `Level` node, connecting it to the HUD's `_on_score_changed`.

Alternative method: Note that if you don't want to use the scene tree to connect the signals, or if you find the signal connection window confusing, you can accomplish the same thing in code by adding these two lines to the `_ready()` function of `Level.gd`:

```
$Player.connect('life_changed', $CanvasLayer/HUD,
                '_on_Player_life_changed')
$Player.connect('dead', self, '_on_Player_dead')
connect('score_changed', $CanvasLayer/HUD, '_on_score_changed')
```

Run your level and verify that you gain points when collecting items and lose hearts when getting hurt.

Title screen

The title screen is the first scene the player will see. When the player dies, the game will return to this scene and allow you to restart.

Scene setup

Start with a `Control` node and set the **Layout** to **Full Rect**.

Add a `TextureRect`. Set its **Texture** to
`res://assets/environment/layers/back.png`, **Layout** to **Full Rect**, and **Stretch Mode** to **Keep Aspect Covered**.

Add another `TextureRect`, this time with the **Texture** using
`res://assets/environment/layers/middle.png` and the **Stretch Mode** set to **Tile**. Drag the width of the rectangle until it's wider than the screen and arrange it so it covers the bottom half of the screen.

Next, add two `Label` nodes (`Title` and `Message`) and set their **Custom Font** settings using the same options you used earlier for the score label. Set their **Text** properties to **Jungle Jump** and **Press Space to Play**, respectively. When you're finished, the screen should look like this:

To make the title screen a bit more interesting, add an `AnimationPlayer` node and create a new animation. Name it `anim` and set it to autoplay. In this animation, you can animate the various components of the screen to make them move, appear, fade in, or any other effect you like.

Drag the **Title** label to a position above the top of the screen and add a keyframe. Then, drag it back (or manually type the values in **Position**) and set another keyframe at around `0.5` seconds. Feel free to add tracks that are animating the other nodes' properties.

For example, here is an animation that drops the title down, fades in the two textures, and then makes the message appear (note the names of the properties that are modified by each track):

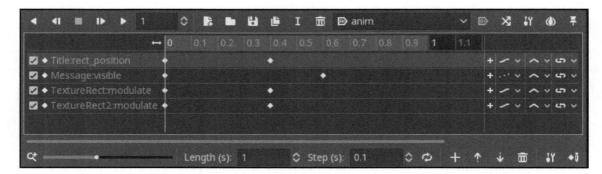

Main scene

Delete the extra nodes you added to your temporary `Main.tscn` (the `Player` instance and the test `StaticBody2D`). This scene will now be responsible for loading the current level. Before it can do that, however, you need an Autoload script to track the game state: variables such as `current_level` and other data that needs to be carried from scene to scene.

Add a new script called `GameState.gd` in the Script editor and add the following code:

```
extends Node

var num_levels = 2
var current_level = 1

var game_scene = 'res://Main.tscn'
var title_screen = 'res://ui/TitleScreen.tscn'

func restart():
    get_tree().change_scene(title_screen)

func next_level():
    current_level += 1
    if current_level <= num_levels:
        get_tree().reload_current_scene()
```

Note that you should set `num_levels` to the number of levels you've made in the `levels` folder. Make sure to name them consistently (`Level01.tscn`, `Level02.tscn`, and so on) and then you can automatically load the next one in the sequence.

Add this script in the **AutoLoad** tab of **Project Settings**, and add this script to `Main`:

```
extends Node

func _ready():
    # make sure your level numbers are 2 digits ("01", etc.)
    var level_num = str(GameState.current_level).pad_zeros(2)
    var path = 'res://levels/Level%s.tscn' % level_num
    var map = load(path).instance()
    add_child(map)
```

Now, whenever the `Main` scene is loaded, it will load the level scene corresponding to `GameState.current_level`.

The title screen needs to transition to the game scene, so attach this script to the `TitleScreen` node:

```
extends Control

func _input(event):
    if event.is_action_pressed('ui_select'):
        get_tree().change_scene(GameState.game_scene)
```

You can also call the restart function when the player dies by adding it to the method in `Level.gd`:

```
func _on_Player_dead():
    GameState.restart()
```

Level transitions

Your levels now need a way to transition from one to the next. In the `res://assets/environment/layers/props.png` sprite sheet, there is an image of a door that you can use for your level's exit. Finding and walking into the door will result in the player moving to the next level.

Door scene

Make a new scene with an `Area2D` named `Door` and save it in the `items` folder. Add a `Sprite` and use the `res://assets/environment/layers/props.png` sprite sheet along with the *Region* setting to select the door image, then attach a rectangular `CollisionShape2D`. This scene doesn't need a script, because you're just going to use the area's `body_entered` signal.

Put the door on the `collectibles` layer and set its mask to only scan the `player` layer.

Instance this door scene in your first level and put it somewhere that the player can reach. Click on the `Door` node and connect the `body_entered` signal to the `Level.gd` script where you can add this code:

```
func _on_Door_body_entered(body):
    GameState.next_level()
```

Run the game and try running into the door to check that it immediately transfers to the next level.

Finishing touches

Now that you've completed the structure of the game, you can consider some additions so that you can add more game features, more visual effects, additional enemies, or other ideas you might have. In this section, there are a few suggested features—add them as-is or adjust them to your liking.

Sound effects

As with the previous projects, you can add audio effects and music to improve the gameplay experience. In the `res://assets/audio` folder, you'll find a number of files you can use for various game events, such as player jump, enemy hit and pickup. There are also two music files: Intro Theme for the title screen and Grasslands Theme for the level scenes.

Adding these to the game will be left to you, but here are a few tips:

- Make sure the sound effects have **Loop** set to **Off** while the music files have it **On** in the **Import** settings tab.

- You may find it helpful to adjust the volume of individual sounds. This can be set with the **Volume Db** property. Setting a negative value will reduce the sound's volume.
- You can attach music to the master `Level.tscn` and that music will be used for all levels (set the `AudioStreamPlayer` to **Autoplay**).
- You an also attach separate music to individual levels if you want to set a certain mood.

Infinite falling

Depending on how you've designed your levels, it may be possible for the player to fall off the level entirely. Typically, you want to design things so that this isn't possible by using walls that are too high to jump, spikes at the bottom of pits, and so on. However, in case it does happen, add the following code to the player's `_physics_process()` method:

```
if position.y > 1000:
    change_state(DEAD)
```

Note that if you've designed a level that extends below a `y` of `1000`, you'll need to increase the value to prevent accidental death.

Double jump

Double-jumps are a popular platforming feature. The player gets a second, usually smaller, upwards boost if they press the jump key a second time while in the air. To implement this feature, you need to add a few things to the player script.

First, you will need two variables to track the state:

```
var max_jumps = 2
var jump_count = 0
```

When entering the JUMP state, reset the number of jumps:

```
JUMP:
    new_anim = 'jump_up'
    jump_count = 1
```

Finally, in `get_input()`, allow the jump if it meets the conditions:

```
if jump and state == JUMP and jump_count < max_jumps:
    new_anim = 'jump_up'
    velocity.y = jump_speed / 1.5
    jump_count += 1
```

Note that this makes the second jump 2/3 the upward speed of the normal jump. You can adjust this according to your preferences.

Dust particles

Dust particles at the character's feet are a low-effort effect that can add a lot of character to your player's movements. In this section, you'll add a small puff of dust to the player's feet that is emitted whenever they land on the ground. This adds a sense of weight and impact to the player's jumps.

Add a `Particles2D` node and name it `Dust`. Note the warning that a process material must be added. First, however, set the properties of the `Dust` node:

Property	Value
Amount	20
Lifetime	0.45
One Shot	On
Speed Scale	2
Explosiveness	0.7
Local Coords	Off
Position	(-2, 15)
Rotation	-90

Now, under **Process Material**, add a new `ParticlesMaterial`. Click on it and you'll see all the particle settings. Here are the ones you need for the dust effect:

Particle Property	Value
Emission Shape	Box
Box Extents	(1, 6, 1)
Gravity	(0, 0, 0)
Initial Velocity	10
Velocity Random	1

Scale	5
Scale Random	1

The default particle color is white, but the dust effect will look better as a tan shade. It should also fade away so that it appears to dissipate. This can be accomplished with a `ColorRamp`. Next to **Color Ramp**, click on **New GradientTexture**. In the `GradientTexture` properties, choose a new `Gradient`.

The `Gradient` has two colors: a start color on the left and an end color on the right. These are selected by the small rectangles at the ends of the gradient. Clicking on the square on the right allows you to set the color:

Set the start color to a tan shade, and set the end color to the same color, but with the alpha value set to 0 (transparent). You can test how it looks by checking the **Emitting** box in the **Inspector**. Because the node is set to **One Shot**, there will only be one puff of particles and you have to check the box again to emit them.

Feel free to alter the properties from what is listed here. Experimenting with `Particles2D` settings can be great fun, and often you'll stumble on to a very nice effect just by tinkering. Once you're happy with the appearance, add the following to the Player's `_physics_process()` code:

```
if state == JUMP and is_on_floor():
    change_state(IDLE)
    $Dust.emitting = true # add this line
```

Run the game and every time your character lands on the ground, a small puff of dust will appear.

Crouching state

The crouching state is useful if you have enemies or projectiles that the player needs to dodge by ducking under them. The sprite sheet contains a two-frame animation for this state:

Add a new animation called **crouch** to the player's `AnimationPlayer`. Set its **Length** to `0.2` and add a track for the **Frame** property that changes the value from `3` to `4`. Set the animation to loop.

In the player's script, add the new state to the `enum` and state change:

```
enum {IDLE, RUN, JUMP, HURT, DEAD, CROUCH}

CROUCH:
    new_anim = 'crouch'
```

In the `get_input()` method, you need to handle the various state transitions. When on the ground, the down input should transition to CROUCH. When in CROUCH, releasing the down input should transition to IDLE. Finally, if in the CROUCH state and left or right is pressed, the state should change to RUN:

```
var down = Input.is_action_pressed('crouch')

if down and is_on_floor():
    change_state(CROUCH)
if !down and state == CROUCH:
    change_state(IDLE)
```

You also need to change this line:

```
if state == IDLE and velocity.x != 0:
    change_state(RUN)
```

To this:

```
if state in [IDLE, CROUCH] and velocity.x != 0:
    change_state(RUN)
```

That's it! Run the game and try out your new animation state.

Climbing ladders

The player animation also includes frames for a *climbing* action, and the tileset contains ladders. Currently, the ladder tiles do nothing: in the **TileSet**, they do not have any collision shape assigned. That's fine, because you don't want the player to collide with the ladders; you want to be able to move up and down on them.

Player code

Start by clicking on the player's AnimationPlayer and adding a new animation named climb. Its **Length** should be set to 0.4 seconds and the **Frame** values for the Sprite are 0, 1, 0, 2. Set the animation to loop.

Now, go to Player.gd and add a new state, CLIMB, to the state enum. In addition, add two new variables to the declarations at the top:

```
export (int) var climb_speed
var is_on_ladder = false
```

is_on_ladder will be used to tell if the player is on a ladder or not. Using this, you can decide whether the up arrow should have any effect. In the **Inspector**, set **Climb Speed** to 50.

In change_state(), add a condition for the new state:

```
CLIMB:
    new_anim = 'climb'
```

Next, in _get_input(), you need to add the climb input action and add the code to determine when to trigger the new state. Add the following:

```
var climb = Input.is_action_pressed('climb')

if climb and state != CLIMB and is_on_ladder:
    change_state(CLIMB)
if state == CLIMB:
```

```
        if climb:
            velocity.y = -climb_speed
        elif down:
            velocity.y = climb_speed
        else:
            velocity.y = 0
            $AnimationPlayer.play("climb")
    if state == CLIMB and not is_on_ladder:
        change_state(IDLE)
```

Here, you have three new conditions to check. First, if the player is not in the CLIMB state, but is on a ladder, then pressing up should start make the player start climbing. Next, if the player is climbing, then up and down should move them accordingly, but halt movement if no keys are pressed. Finally, if the player leaves the ladder while climbing, it will leave the CLIMB state.

The one remaining issue is you need gravity to stop pulling the player downwards when climbing. Add the following condition to the gravity code in _physics_process():

```
    if state != CLIMB:
        velocity.y += gravity * delta
```

Now, the player is ready, and you can add some ladders to your level map.

Level code

Place a few ladder tiles somewhere on your map, then add a Ladder Area2D to the level scene. Give this node a CollisionShape2D with a rectangular shape. The best way to size the area is to use grid snapping. Turn this on via the menu and use **Configure Snap...** to set the grid step to (4, 4):

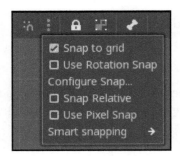

Adjust the collision shape so that it covers the center portion of the ladder from top to bottom. If you make the shape fully as wide as the ladder, the player will still count as climbing even when hanging off the side. You may find that this looks a bit odd, so making the shape a bit smaller than the width of the ladder will prevent this.

Connect the `body_entered` and `body_exited` signals of the `Ladder` and add the following code to have them set the Player's ladder variable:

```
func _on_Ladder_body_entered(body):
    if body.name == "Player":
        body.is_on_ladder = true

func _on_Ladder_body_exited(body):
    if body.name == "Player":
        body.is_on_ladder = false
```

Now you can give it a try. You should be able to walk to the ladder and climb up and down it. Note that if you are at the top of a ladder and step onto it, you'll fall to the bottom rather than climb down (although pressing up as you fall will grab the ladder). If you prefer to automatically transition to the climbing state, you can add an additional falling check in `_physics_process()`.

Moving platforms

Make a new scene with a `KinematicBody2D` root node. Add a `Sprite` child and use the `res://assets/environment/layers/tileset.png` sprite sheet as the **Texture** with **Region** enabled so you can choose one particular tile. You probably want your platform to be wider than one tile, so duplicate the `Sprite` as many times as you like. Turn grid snapping on so that the sprites can be aligned in a row:

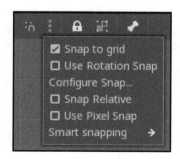

A grid setting of (8, 8) works well for aligning the tiles. Add a rectangular CollisionShape2D that covers the image:

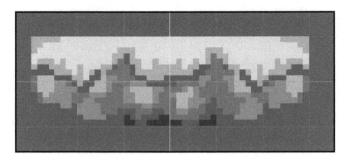

Platform movement can be made very complex (following paths, changing speeds, and so on), but this example will stick with a platform that moves horizontally back and forth between two objects.

Here is the platform's script:

```
extends KinematicBody2D

export (Vector2) var velocity

func _physics_process(delta):
    var collision = move_and_collide(velocity * delta)
    if collision:
        velocity = velocity.bounce(collision.normal)
```

This time, you're using move_and_collide() to move the kinematic body. This is a better choice since the platform shouldn't slide when it collides with another wall. Instead, it bounces off the colliding body. As long as your collision shapes are rectangular (as the TileMap bodies are), this method will work fine. If you have a rounded object, the bounce may send the platform off in a strange direction, in which case you should use something like the following to keep the motion horizontal:

```
func _physics_process(delta):
    var collision = move_and_collide(velocity * delta)
    if collision:
        velocity.x *= -1
```

Set the *Velocity* in the Inspector to (50, 0), then go to your level scene and instance one of these objects somewhere in your level. Make sure it is between two objects so that it can move back and forth between them.

Run the scene and try jumping on the moving platform. Since the Player is using `move_and_slide()`, they will automatically move along with the platform if you stand on it.

Add as many of these objects as you like to your level. They will even bounce off each other, so you can make chains of moving platforms that cover a large distance and require careful timing of the player's jumps.

Summary

In this chapter, you learned how to use the `KinematicBody2D` node to create arcade-style physics. You also used the `AnimationPlayer` to create a variety of animations for character behavior, and made extensive use of what you learned in earlier projects to tie everything together. Hopefully, by this point, you have a good grasp of the scene system and how a Godot project is structured.

Remember the **Stretch Mode** and **Aspect** properties you set in the **Project Settings** at the beginning? Run the game and observe what happens when you resize the game window. These settings are the best for this style of game, but try changing the **Stretch Mode** to **Viewport** instead, then make your game window very wide or tall. Experiment with the other settings to see the effect of the different resizing options.

Once again, before moving on, take a few moments to play your game and look through its various scenes and scripts to review how you built it. Review any sections of this chapter that you found particularly tricky.

In the next chapter, you'll make the jump to 3D!

6
3D Minigolf

The previous projects in this book have been designed in 2D space. This is intentional, in order to introduce the various features and concepts of Godot while keeping the projects' scopes limited. In this chapter, you'll venture into the 3D side of game development. For some, 3D development feels significantly more difficult to manage; for others, it is more straightforward. In either case, there is certainly an additional layer of complexity for you to understand.

If you've never worked with any kind of 3D software before, you may find yourself encountering many new concepts. This chapter will explain them as much as possible, but remember to refer to the Godot documentation whenever you need a more in-depth understanding of a particular topic.

The game you'll make in this chapter is called **Minigolf**. This will consist of a small customizable course, a ball, and an interface for aiming and shooting the ball towards the hole.

This is what you'll learn in this chapter:

- Navigating Godot's 3D editor
- The Spatial node and its properties
- Importing 3D meshes and using 3D collision shapes
- How to use 3D cameras, both stationary and moving
- Using GridMap to place the tiles of your golf course
- Setting up lighting and the environment
- An introduction to PBR rendering and materials

But first, here's a brief introduction to 3D in Godot.

Introduction to 3D

One of the strengths of Godot is its ability to handle both 2D and 3D games. While much of what you've learned earlier in this book applies equally well in 3D (nodes, scenes, signals, and so on), changing from 2D to 3D brings with it a whole new layer of complexity and capabilities. First, you'll find that there are some additional features available in the 3D editor window, and it's a good idea to familiarize yourself with how to navigate in the 3D editor window.

Orienting in 3D space

When you click on the 3D button at the top of the editor window, you will see the 3D project view:

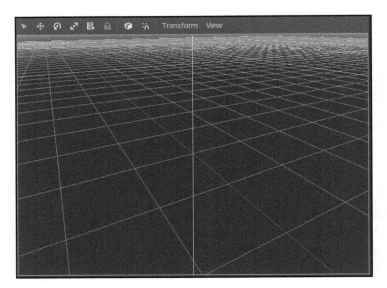

The first thing you should notice is the three colored lines in the center. These are the x (red), y (green), and z (blue) axes. The point where they meet is the origin, with coordinates of `(0, 0, 0)`.

Just as you used `Vector2(x, y)` to indicate a position in two-dimensional space, `Vector3(x, y, z)` describes a position in three dimensions along these three axes.

One issue that arises when working in 3D is that different applications use different conventions for orientation. Godot uses Y-Up orientation, so when looking at the axes, if *x* is pointing to the left/right, then *y* is up/down, and *z* is forward/back. You may find when using other popular 3D software that they use Z-Up. It's good to be aware of this, as it can lead to confusion when moving between different programs.

Another major aspect to be aware of is the unit of measure. In 2D, everything is measured in pixels, which makes sense as a natural basis for measurement when drawing on the screen. However, when working in 3D space, pixels aren't really useful. Two objects of exactly the same size will occupy different areas on the screen depending on how far away they are from the camera (more about cameras soon). For this reason, in 3D space all objects in Godot are measured in generic units. You're free to call these units whatever you like: meters, inches, or even light years, depending on the scale of your game world.

Godot's 3D editor

Before getting started with 3D, it will be useful to briefly review how to navigate in Godot's 3D space. The camera is controlled with the mouse and keyboard:

- Mousewheel up/down: Zoom in/out
- Middle button + drag: Orbit the camera around the current target
- *Shift* + middle button + drag: Pan camera up/down/left/right
- Right-click + drag: Rotate camera in place

If you're familiar with popular 3D games such as *Minecraft*, you can press *Shift* + *F* to switch to Freelook mode. In this mode, you can use the WASD keys to *fly* around the scene while aiming with the mouse. Press *Shift* + *F* again to exit Freelook mode.

You can also alter the camera's view by clicking on the **[Perspective]** label in the upper-left corner. Here, you can snap the camera to a particular orientation such as **Top View** or **Front View**:

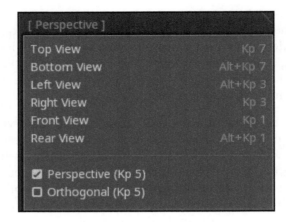

This can be especially useful on large displays when combined with the use of multiple **Viewports**. Click the **View** menu and you can split the screen into multiple views of the space, allowing you to see an object from all sides simultaneously.

 Note that each of these menu options has a keyboard shortcut associated with it. You can click on **Editor** | **Editor Settings** | **3D** to adjust the 3D navigation and shortcuts to your liking.

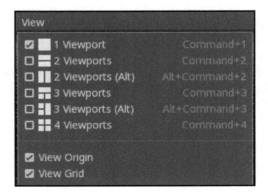

When using multiple viewports, each can be set to a different perspective so you can see the effect of your actions from multiple directions at the same time:

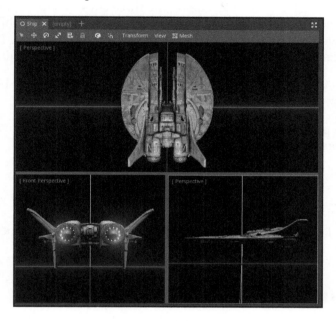

Adding 3D objects

It's time to add your first 3D node. Just as all 2D nodes inherit from `Node2D`, which provides properties such as `position` and `rotation`, 3D nodes inherit from the `Spatial` node. Add one to the scene and you'll see the following:

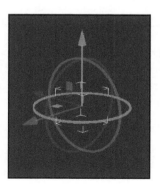

That colorful object you see is not the node, but rather a 3D *gizmo*. Gizmos are tools that allow you to move and rotate objects in space. The three rings control rotation, while the three arrows move (translate) the object along the three axes. Notice that the rings and arrows are color-coded to match the axis colors. The arrows move the object *along* the respective axis, while the rings rotate the object *around* a particular axis. There are also three small squares that lock one axis and allow you to move the object in a single plane.

Take a few minutes to experiment and get familiar with the gizmo. Use Undo if you find yourself getting lost.

Sometimes, gizmos get in the way. You can click on the mode icons to restrict yourself to only one type of transformation: move, rotate, or scale:

The *Q*, *W*, *E*, and *R* keys are shortcuts for these buttons, allowing for quickly changing between modes.

Global versus Local Space

By default, the gizmo controls operate in global space. Try rotating the object. No matter how you turn it, the gizmo's movement arrows still point along the axes. Now try this: put the `Spatial` node back to its original position and orientation (or delete it and add a new one). Rotate the object around one axis, then click the **Local Space Mode (T)** button:

Observe what happened to the gizmo arrows. They now point along the *object's* local *x*/*y*/*z* axes and not the world's. When you click and drag them, they will move the object relative to its axes. Switching back and forth between these two modes can make it much easier to place an object exactly where you want it.

Transforms

Look at the **Inspector** for your `Spatial` node. Instead of a **Position** property, you now have **Translation**, as well as **Rotation Degrees** and **Scale**. As you move the object around, observe how these values change. Note that the **Translation** represents the object's coordinates relative to the origin:

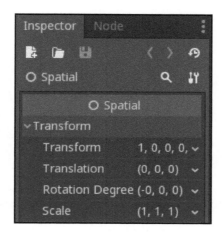

You'll also notice a **Transform** property, which also changes as you move and rotate the object. When you change translation or rotation, you'll notice that the 12 transform quantities will change as well.

A full explanation of the math behind transforms is beyond the scope of this book, but in a nutshell, a transform is a *matrix* that describes an object's translation, rotation, and scale all at once. You briefly used the 2D equivalent in the Space Rocks game earlier in this book, but the concept is more widely applied in 3D.

Transforms in code

When positioning a 3D node via code, you have access to its `transform` and `global_transform` properties, which are `Transform` objects. A `Transform` has two sub-properties: `origin` and `basis`. The `origin` represents the body's offset from its parent's origin or the global origin, respectively. The `basis` property contains three vectors that define a local coordinate system traveling with the object. Think of the three axis arrows in the gizmo when you are in Local Space mode.

You'll see more about how to use 3D transforms later in this section.

Meshes

Just like `Node2D`, a `Spatial` node has no size or appearance of its own. In 2D, you added a Sprite to assign a texture to the node. In 3D, you need to add a *mesh*. A mesh is a mathematical description of a shape. It consists of a collection of points, called *vertices*. These vertices are connected by lines, called *edges*, and multiple edges (at least three) together make a *face*:

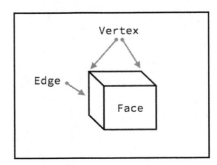

A cube, for example, is composed of eight vertices, twelve edges, and six faces.

If you've ever used 3D design software, this will be very familiar to you. If you haven't, and you're interested in learning about 3D modeling, Blender is a very popular open source tool for designing 3D objects. You can find many tutorials and lessons on the internet to help you get started with Blender.

Importing meshes

Whatever modeling software you may use, you will need to export your models in a format that is readable by Godot. Wavefront (`.obj`) and Collada (`.dae`) are the most popular. Unfortunately, if you're using Blender, its Collada exporter has some flaws that make it unusable with Godot. To fix this, Godot's developers have created a Blender plugin called **Better Collada Exporter** that you can download from https://godotengine.org/download.

If your objects are in another format, such as FBX, you'll need to use a converter tool to save them as OBJ or DAE in order to use them with Godot.

 A new format called GLTF is gaining in popularity and has some significant advantages over Collada. Godot already supports it, so feel free to experiment with any models you may find in this format.

Primitives

If you don't have any models handy, or if you just need a simple model quickly, Godot has the ability to create certain 3D meshes directly. Add a `MeshInstance` node as a child of Spatial, and in the **Inspector**, click the **Mesh** property:

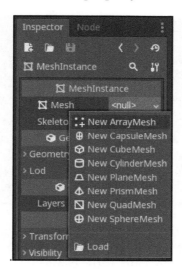

These predefined shapes are called *primitives* and they represent a handy collection of common useful shapes. You can use these shapes for a variety of purposes, as you'll see later in this chapter. Select **New CubeMesh** and you'll see a plain cube appear on the screen. The cube itself is white, but it may appear bluish on your screen due to the default ambient light in the 3D editor window. You'll learn how to work with lighting later in this chapter.

Multiple meshes

Often, you'll find yourself with an object composed of many different meshes. A character might have separate meshes for its head, torso, and limbs. If you have a great many of these types of objects, it can lead to performance issues as the engine tries to render so many meshes. As a result, `MultiMeshInstance` is designed to provide a high-performance method of grouping many meshes together into a single object. You probably don't need it yet, because it won't be necessary for this project, but keep it in mind as a tool that may come in handy later.

Cameras

Try running the scene with your cube mesh. Where is it? In 3D, you won't see anything in the game viewport without using a `Camera`. Add one, and use the camera's gizmo to position and point it towards the cube, as in the following screenshot:

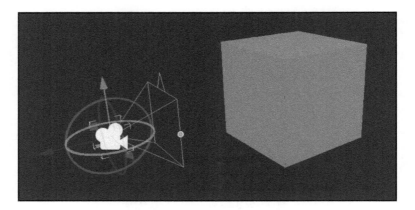

The pinkish-purple, pyramid-shaped object is called the camera's *fustrum*. It represents the camera's view, and can be made narrow or wide to affect the camera's *field of view*. The triangular arrow at the top of the fustrum is the camera's up direction.

As you're moving the camera around, you can use the **Preview** button in the upper-right to check your aim. **Preview** will always show you what the selected camera can see.

As with the `Camera2D` you used earlier, a `Camera` must be set as **Current** for it to be active. Its other properties affect how it *sees*: field of view, projection, and near/far. The default values of these properties are good for this project, but go ahead and experiment with them to see how they affect the view of the cube. Use Undo to return everything to the default values when you're done.

Project setup

Now that you've learned how to navigate in Godot's 3D editor, you're ready to start on the Minigolf project. As with the other projects, download the game assets from the following link and unzip them in your project folder. The unzipped `assets` folder contains images, 3D models, and the other assets you need to complete the project. You can download a Zip file of the art and sounds (collectively known as *assets*) for the game here, https://github. com/PacktPublishing/Godot-Game-Engine-Projects/releases.

This game will use the left mouse button as an input. The Input Map does not have any default actions defined for this, so you need to add one. Open **Project | Project Settings** and go to the **Input Map** tab. Add a new action called **click**, then click the plus to add a **Mouse Button** event to it. Choose **Left Button**:

Creating the course

For the first scene, add a node called `Main` to serve as your scene's root. This scene will contain the major parts of the game, starting with the course itself. Start by adding a `GridMap` node to lay out the course.

GridMaps

`GridMap` is the 3D equivalent of the `TileMap` node you used in earlier projects. It allows you to use a collection of meshes (contained in a `MeshLibrary`) and lay them out in a grid to more quickly design an environment. Because it is 3D, you can stack the meshes in any direction, although for this project, you'll stick to the same plane.

Making a MeshLibrary

The `res://assets` folder contains a pre-generated `MeshLibrary` for the project, containing all the necessary course parts along with collision shapes. However, if you need to change it or make your own, you'll find the procedure is very similar to how `TileSet` is created in 2D.

The scene used to create the pre-generated `MeshLibrary` can also be found in the `res://assets` folder. Its name is `course_tiles_edit1.tscn`. Feel free to open it and look at how it is set up.

Start by making a new scene, with a `Spatial` as its root. To this node, add any number of `MeshInstance`. You can find the original course meshes, exported from Blender, in the `res://assets/dae` folder.

The names you give to these nodes will be their names in the `MeshLibrary`.

Once you have added the meshes, they need static collision bodies added to them. Creating collision shapes that match a given mesh can be complicated, but Godot has a method of automatically generating them.

Select a mesh and you'll see a `Mesh` menu appear at the top of the editor window:

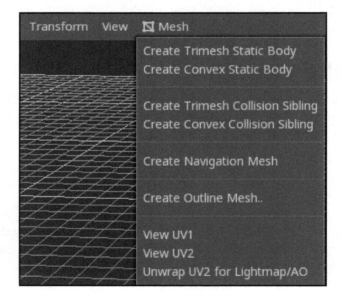

Select **Create Trimesh Static Body** and Godot will create a `StaticBody` and add a `CollisionShape` using the mesh's data:

Do this with each of your mesh objects, and then select **Scene | Convert To | MeshLibrary** to save the resource.

Drawing the course

Drag the `MeshLibrary` (`res://assets/course_tiles.tres` or the one you created) into the **Theme** property of `GridMap` in the **Inspector**. Also, check that the **Cell/Size** property is set to (2, 2, 2):

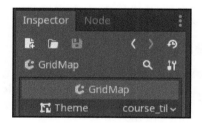

Try drawing by selecting the tile piece from the list on the right and placing it by left-clicking in the editor window. You can rotate a piece around the y axis by pressing *S*. To remove a tile, use *Shift* + right-click.

For now, stick to a simple course; you can get fancy later when everything is working. Don't forget the hole!

Now, it's time to see what this is going to look like when the game is run. Add a `Camera` to the scene. Move it up and angle it so it looks down on the course. Remember, you can use the Preview button to check what the camera sees.

Run the scene. You'll see that everything seems very dark. By default, there is minimal environmental light in the scene. To see more clearly, you need to add more light.

WorldEnvironment

Lighting is a complex subject all on its own. Deciding where to place lights and how to set their color and intensity can dramatically affect how a scene looks.

Godot provides three lighting nodes in 3D:

- `OmniLight`: For light that is emitted in all directions, like from a light bulb or candle
- `DirectionalLight`: Infinite light from a distant source, such as sunlight
- `SpotLight`: Directional light from a single source, such as a flashlight

In addition to using individual lights, you can also set an *ambient* light using `WorldEnvironment`.

Add a `WorldEnvironment` node to the scene. In the Inspector, select **New Environment** in the **Environment** property. Everything will turn black, but don't worry, you'll fix that soon:

Click on **New Environment** and you'll see a large list of properties. The one you want is **Ambient Light**. Set **Color** to white and you'll see your scene become more brightly lit.

 Keep in mind that ambient light comes from all directions equally. If your scene needs shadows or other light effects, you'll want to use one of the `Light` nodes. You'll see how light nodes work later in the chapter.

Finishing the scene

Now that you have the course laid out, two more items remain: the *tee,* or location where the ball will start, and a way to detect when the ball has entered the hole.

Add a `Position3D` node named `Tee`. Just like `Position2D`, this node is used to mark a location in space. Place this node where you want the ball to start. Make sure you put it just above the surface so that the ball doesn't spawn inside the ground.

To detect the ball entering the hole, you can use an `Area` node. This node is directly analogous to the 2D version: it can signal when a body enters its assigned shape. Add an `Area` and give it a `CollisionShape` child.

In the child's **Shape** property of the `CollisionShape`, add a `SphereShape`:

To size the collision sphere, use the single radius adjustment handle:

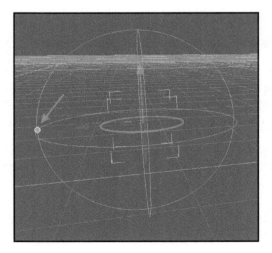

Place the `Area` just below the hole and size the collision shape so that it overlaps the bottom of the hole. Don't let it project above the top of the hole, or the ball will count as *in* when it hasn't dropped in yet.

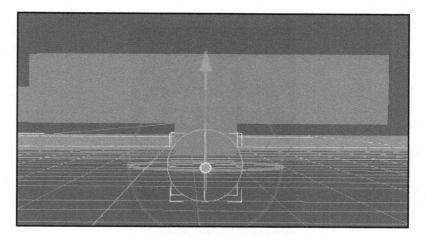

You may find it easier to position the node if you use the Perspective button to view the hole from one direction at at time. When you've finished positioning it, change the name of the `Area` to `Hole`.

Ball

Now, you're ready to make the ball. Since the ball needs physics—gravity, friction, collision with walls, and other physics properties—`RigidBody` will be the best choice of node. Create a new scene with a `RigidBody` named `Ball`.

`RigidBody` is the 3D equivalent of the `RigidBody2D` node you used in `Chapter 3`, *Escape the Maze*. Its behavior and properties are very similar, and you use many of the same methods to interact with it, such as `apply_impulse()` and `_integrate_forces()`.

The shape of the ball needs to be a sphere. The basic 3D shapes such as sphere, cube, cylinder, and so on are called *primitives*. Godot can automatically make primitives using the `MeshInstance` node, so add one as a child of the body. In the **Inspector**, choose **New SphereMesh** in the **Mesh** property:

The default size is much too large, so click on the new sphere mesh and set its size properties, **Radius** to `0.15` and **Height** to `0.3`:

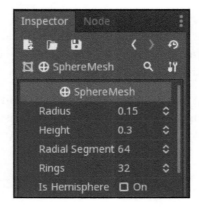

Next, add a `CollisionShape` node to the `Ball` and give it a `SphereShape`. Size it to fit the mesh using the size handle (orange dot):

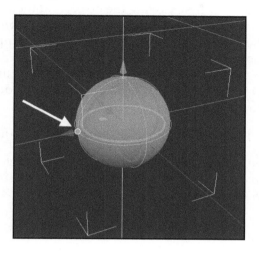

Testing the ball

To test the ball, add it to the `Main` scene with the instance button. Position it somewhere above the course and hit Play. You should see the ball fall and land on the ground. You may find it helpful to add another `Camera` node positioned on the side of the course for a different view. Set the **Current** property on whichever camera you want to use.

You can also temporarily give the ball some motion by setting its **Linear/Velocity** property. Try setting it to different values and playing the scene. Remember that the *y* axis is up and that using too large a value may cause the ball to go right through the wall. Set it back to (0, 0, 0) when you're done.

Improving collisions

You may have noticed when adjusting the velocity that the ball sometimes goes straight through the wall and/or bounces oddly, especially if you choose a high value. There are a few adjustments you can make to the `RigidBody` properties to improve the collision behavior at high speeds.

First, turn on **Continuous Collision Detection** (**CCD**). You'll find it listed as **Continuous Cd** in the **Inspector**. Using CCD alters the way the physics engine calculates collisions. Normally, the engine operates by first moving the object and then testing for and resolving collisions. This is fast, and works in most common situations. When using CCD, however, the engine projects the object's movement along its path and attempts to predict where the collision may occur. This is slower than the default behavior, and so not as efficient, especially when simulating many objects, but it is much more accurate. Since you only have one ball in the game, CCD is a good option because it won't introduce any noticeable performance penalty, but will greatly improve collision detection.

The ball also needs a little more action, so set the **Bounce** to 0.2 and the **Gravity Scale** to 2.

Finally, you may also have noticed that the ball takes a long time to come to a stop. Set the **Linear/Damp** property to 0.5 and **Angular/Damp** to 0.1 so that you won't have to wait as long for the ball to stop moving.

UI

Now that the ball is on the course, you need a way to aim and hit the ball. There are a number of possible control schemes for a game of this type. For this project, you'll use a two-step process:

1. Aim: An arrow will appear swinging back and forth. Clicking the mouse button will set the aim direction to the arrow's.
2. Shoot: A power bar will move up and down on the screen. Clicking the mouse will set the power and launch the ball.

Aiming arrow

Drawing an object in 3D is not as easy as it is in 2D. In many cases, you'll have to switch to a 3D modeling program such as Blender to create your game's objects. However, in this case Godot's primitives have you covered; to make an arrow, you just need two meshes: a long, thin rectangle and a triangular prism.

Start a new scene by adding a `Spatial` node with a `MeshInstance` child. Add a new `CubeMesh`. Click on the **Mesh** property and set the **Size** property to (0.5, 0.2, 2). This is the body of the arrow, but it still has one problem. If you rotate the parent, the mesh rotates around its center. Instead, you need the arrow to rotate around its end, so change the **Transform/Translation** of **MeshInstance** to (0, 0, -1):

Try rotating the `Arrow` (root) node with the gizmo to confirm that the shape is now offset correctly.

To create the point of the arrow, add another `MeshInstance`, and this time choose **New PrismMesh**. Set its size to `(1.5, 2, 0.5)`. You now have a flat triangle shape. To place it properly at the end of the rectangle, change the mesh's **Transform/Translation** to `(0, 0, -3)` and its **Rotation Degrees** to `(-90, 0, 0)`.

 Using primitives is a quick way to create placeholder objects directly in Godot without having to open up your 3D modeling software.

Finally, scale the whole arrow down by setting the root node's **Transform/Scale** to (0.5, 0.5, 0.5):

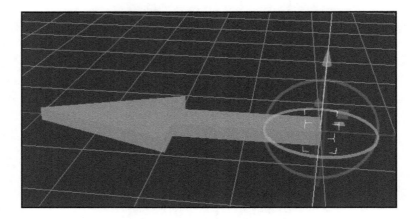

You now have a completed arrow shape. Save it, then instance it in the Main scene.

UI display

Create a new scene with a **CanvasLayer** called UI. In this scene, you'll show the power bar as well as the shot count for the player's score. Add a MarginContainer, VBoxContainer, two Label properties, and a TextureProgress. Name them as shown:

Set the **Custom Constants** of MarginContainer all to 20. Add the Xolonium-Regular.ttf font to both of the Label nodes and set their font sizes to 30. Set the Shots label's **Text** to **Shots: 0** and the Label **Text** to **Power**. Drag one of the colored bar textures from res://assets into the **Texture/Progress** of PowerBar. By default, TextureProgress bars grow from left to right, so for a vertical orientation, change the **Fill Mode** to **Bottom to Top**.

The completed UI layout should look like this:

Instance this scene in the Main scene. Because it's a CanvasLayer, it will be drawn on top of the 3D camera view.

Scripts

In this section, you'll create the scripts needed to make everything work together. The flow of the game will be as follows:

1. Place the ball at the start (Tee)
2. Angle mode: Aim the ball
3. Power mode: Set the hit power
4. Launch the ball
5. Repeat from step 2 until the ball is in the hole

UI

Add the following script to the UI to update the UI elements:

```
extends CanvasLayer

var bar_red = preload("res://assets/bar_red.png")
var bar_green = preload("res://assets/bar_green.png")
var bar_yellow = preload("res://assets/bar_yellow.png")

func update_shots(value):
    $Margin/Container/Shots.text = 'Shots: %s' % value

func update_powerbar(value):
    $Margin/Container/PowerBar.texture_progress = bar_green
    if value > 70:
        $Margin/Container/PowerBar.texture_progress = bar_red
    elif value > 40:
        $Margin/Container/PowerBar.texture_progress = bar_yellow
    $Margin/Container/PowerBar.value = value
```

The two functions provide a way to update the UI elements when they need to display a new value. As you did in the Space Rocks game, changing the progress bar's texture based on its size gives a nice high/medium/low feel to the power level.

Main

Next, add a script to Main and start with these variables:

```
extends Node

var shots = 0
var state
var power = 0
var power_change = 1
var power_speed = 100
var angle_change = 1
var angle_speed = 1.1
enum {SET_ANGLE, SET_POWER, SHOOT, WIN}
```

The enum lists the states the game can be in, while the power* and angle* variables will be used to set their respective values and change them over time. Take a look at the following code snippet:

```
func _ready():
    $Arrow.hide()
    $Ball.transform.origin = $Tee.transform.origin
    change_state(SET_ANGLE)
```

At the beginning, the ball is placed at the location of the Tee using both bodies' transform.origin properties. Then, the game is put into the SET_ANGLE state:

```
func change_state(new_state):
    state = new_state
    match state:
        SET_ANGLE:
            $Arrow.transform.origin = $Ball.transform.origin
            $Arrow.show()
        SET_POWER:
            pass
        SHOOT:
            $Arrow.hide()
            $Ball.shoot($Arrow.rotation.y, power)
            shots += 1
            $UI.update_shots(shots)
        WIN:
            $Ball.hide()
            $Arrow.hide()
```

The SET_ANGLE state places the arrow at the ball's location. Recall that you offset the arrow, so it will appear to be pointing out from the ball. When rotating the arrow, you rotate it around the *y* axis so that it remains flat (the *y* axis points upwards).

Also, note that when entering the SHOOT state, you call the shoot() function on the Ball. You'll add that function in the next section.

The next step is to check for user input:

```
func _input(event):
    if event.is_action_pressed('click'):
        match state:
            SET_ANGLE:
                change_state(SET_POWER)
            SET_POWER:
                change_state(SHOOT)
```

The only input for the game is clicking the left mouse button. Depending on what state you're in, clicking it will transition to the next state:

```
func _process(delta):
    match state:
        SET_ANGLE:
            animate_angle(delta)
        SET_POWER:
            animate_power_bar(delta)
        SHOOT:
            pass
```

In `_process()`, you determine what to animate based on the state. For now, it just calls the function that animates the property that's currently being set:

```
func animate_power_bar(delta):
    power += power_speed * power_change * delta
    if power >= 100:
        power_change = -1
    if power <= 0:
        power_change = 1
    $UI.update_powerbar(power)

func animate_angle(delta):
    $Arrow.rotation.y += angle_speed * angle_change * delta
    if $Arrow.rotation.y > PI/2:
        angle_change = -1
    if $Arrow.rotation.y < -PI/2:
        angle_change = 1
```

Both of these functions are similar. They gradually change a value between two extremes, reversing direction when a limit is hit. Note that the arrow is animating over a +/- 90-degree arc.

Ball

In the ball script, there are two functions needed. First, an impulse must be applied to the ball to launch it. Second, when the ball stops moving, it needs to notify the `Main` scene so that the player can take another shot:

```
extends RigidBody

signal stopped

func shoot(angle, power):
```

```
    var force = Vector3(0, 0, -1).rotated(Vector3(0, 1, 0), angle)
    apply_impulse(Vector3(), force * power / 5)

func _integrate_forces(state):
    if state.linear_velocity.length() < 0.1:
        emit_signal("stopped")
        state.linear_velocity = Vector3()
```

As you saw in the Space Rocks game, you can use the physics state in `_integrate_forces()` to safely stop the ball if the speed has gotten too slow. Remember, due to floating point number precision, the velocity may not actually slow to 0 on its own. The ball may appear to be stopped, but its velocity may actually be something like `0.0000001` instead. Rather than wait for it to reach 0, you can make the ball stop if its speed drops below `0.1`.

Hole

To detect when the ball has dropped into the hole, click on the `Area` in `Main` and connect its `body_entered` signal:

```
func _on_Hole_body_entered(body):
    print("Win!")
    change_state(WIN)
```

Changing to the `WIN` state will prevent the ball's `stopped` signal from allowing another shot.

Testing it out

Try running the game. You may want to make sure you have a very easy course with a straight shot to the hole for this part. You should see the arrow rotating at the ball's position. When you click the mouse button, the arrow stops, and the power bar starts moving up and down. When you click a second time, the ball is launched.

If any of those steps don't work, don't go any further, but stop and go back to try and find what you missed.

Once everything is working, you'll notice some areas that need improvement. First, when the ball stops moving the arrow may not point in the direction you want. The reason for this is that the starting angle is always 0, which points along the z axis, and then the arrow swings +/- 90 degrees from there. In the next sections, you'll have the option of improving the aiming in two ways.

Improving aiming – option 1

The aim could be improved by making the 180-degree swing of the arrow always begin by pointing towards the hole.

Add a variable called `hole_dir` to the `Main` script. At the start of aiming, this will be set to the angle pointing towards the hole using the following function:

```
func set_start_angle():
    var hole_pos = Vector2($Hole.transform.origin.z,
$Hole.transform.origin.x)
    var ball_pos = Vector2($Ball.transform.origin.z,
$Ball.transform.origin.x)
    hole_dir = (ball_pos - hole_pos).angle()
    $Arrow.rotation.y = hole_dir
```

Remember that the ball's position is its center, so it's slightly above the surface, while the hole's center is somewhat below. Because of this, an arrow pointing directly between them would point at a downward angle into the ground. To prevent this and keep the arrow level, you can use only the *x* and *z* values from the `transform.origin` to produce a `Vector2`.

Now the initial arrow direction is towards the hole, so you can alter the animation to add +/-90 degrees to that angle:

```
func animate_angle(delta):
    $Arrow.rotation.y += angle_speed * angle_change * delta
    if $Arrow.rotation.y > hole_dir + PI/2:
        angle_change = -1
    if $Arrow.rotation.y < hole_dir - PI/2:
        angle_change = 1
```

Lastly, change the `SET_ANGLE` state to call the function:

```
SET_ANGLE:
    $Arrow.transform.origin = $Ball.transform.origin
    $Arrow.show()
    set_start_angle()
```

Try the game again. The ball should now always point in the general direction of the hole. This is better, but you still can't point in any direction you like. For that, you can try aiming option 2.

Improving aiming – option 2

The previous solution is acceptable, but there is another possibility. Instead of the arrow bouncing back and forth, you can aim by moving the mouse side-to-side. The benefit of this option is that you're not limited to 180 degrees of motion.

To accomplish this, you can make use of a particular input event: InputEventMouseMotion. This event occurs when the mouse moves, and returns with it a relative property representing how far the mouse moved in the previous frame. You can use this value to rotate the arrow by a small amount.

First, disable the arrow animation by removing the SET_ANGLE portion from _process(). Next, add the following code to _input():

```
func _input(event):
    if event is InputEventMouseMotion:
        if state == SET_ANGLE:
            $Arrow.rotation.y -= event.relative.x / 150
```

This sets the arrow's rotation as you move the mouse left/right on the screen. Dividing by 150 ensures that the movement isn't too fast and that you can move a full 360 degrees if you move the mouse all the way from one side of the screen to the other. Depending on your mouse's sensitivity, you can adjust this to your preference.

Camera improvements

Another problem, especially if you have a relatively large course, is that if your camera is placed to show the starting area near the tee, it may not show the other parts of the course well, or at all. This can make it challenging to aim when the ball is in certain places.

In this section, you'll learn two different ways to address this problem. One involves creating multiple cameras and activating whichever one is closer to the ball's position. The other solution is to create an *orbiting* camera that follows the ball and that the player can control to view the course from any angle.

Multiple cameras

Add a second `Camera` node and position it near the hole or at the opposite end of your course, for example:

Add an `Area` child to this second camera. Name it `Camera2Area` and then add a `CollisionShape`. You could use a spherical shape just as well, but for this example, choose a `BoxShape`. Note that because you've rotated the camera, the box is rotated as well. You can reverse this by setting the rotation of `CollisionShape` to the opposite value, or you can leave it rotated. Either way, adjust the size and position of the box to cover the portion of the course you want the camera to be responsible for:

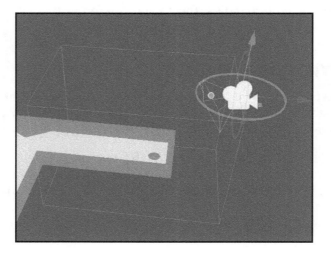

Now, connect the area's `body_entered` signal to the main script. When the ball enters the area, the signal will be emitted, and you can change the active camera:

```
func _on_Cam2Area_body_entered(body):
    $Camera2.current = true
```

Play the game again and hit the ball toward the new camera area. Confirm that the camera view changes when the ball enters the area. For a large course, you can add as many cameras as you want/need and set them to activate for different sections of the course.

The drawback of this method is that the cameras are still static. Unless you've very carefully placed them in the right positions, it still may not be comfortable to aim the ball from some locations on the course.

Orbiting camera

In many 3D games, the player can control a camera that rotates and moves as desired. Typically, the control scheme uses a combination of mouse and keyboard. The first step will be to add some new input actions:

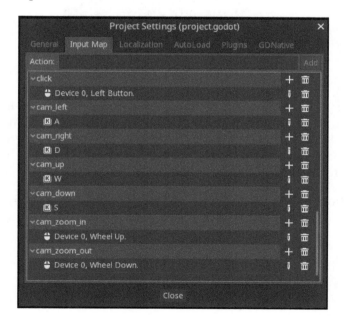

The WASD keys will be used to orbit the camera by moving it side to side and up and down. The mouse wheel will control zooming in/out.

Creating a gimbal

The camera movement needs to have some restrictions. For one, it should always remain level, and not be tilted side to side. Try this: take a camera and rotate it a small amount around x (red ring), then a small amount around z (blue ring). Now, reverse the *x* rotation and click the Preview button. Do you see how the camera is now tilted?

The solution to this problem is to place the camera on a *gimbal*—a device designed to keep an object level during movement. You can create a gimbal using two Spatial nodes, which will control the camera's left/right and up/down movement respectively.

First, make sure to remove any other Camera nodes in the scene. If you tried the multiple camera setup from the previous section and you'd rather not delete them, you can set their **Current** values to **Off** and disconnect any Area signals for them.

Add a new Spatial node called GimbalOut and place it near the center of the course. Make sure not to rotate it. Give it a Spatial child called GimbalIn, and then add a Camera to that node. Set the **Transform/Translation** of **Camera** to (0, 0, 10):

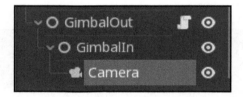

Here's how the gimbal works: the outer spatial is allowed to rotate *only* in *y*, while the inner one rotates *only* in *x*. You can try it yourself, but make sure you change to **Local Space Mode** (see the *Introduction to 3D* section). Remember to only move the *green* ring of the outer gimbal node and only the *red* ring of the inner one. Don't change the camera at all. Reset all the rotations to 0 once you've finished experimenting.

To control this motion in the game, attach a script to GimbalOut and add the following:

```
extends Spatial

var cam_speed = PI/2
var zoom_speed = 0.1
var zoom = 0.5

func _input(event):
    if event.is_action_pressed('cam_zoom_in'):
        zoom -= zoom_speed
    if event.is_action_pressed('cam_zoom_out'):
```

```
            zoom += zoom_speed

func _process(delta):
    zoom = clamp(zoom, 0.1, 2)
    scale = Vector3(1, 1, 1) * zoom
    if Input.is_action_pressed('cam_left'):
        rotate_y(-cam_speed * delta)
    if Input.is_action_pressed('cam_right'):
        rotate_y(cam_speed * delta)
    if Input.is_action_pressed('cam_up'):
        $GimbalIn.rotate_x(-cam_speed * delta)
    if Input.is_action_pressed('cam_down'):
        $GimbalIn.rotate_x(cam_speed * delta)
    $GimbalIn.rotation.x = clamp($GimbalIn.rotation.x, -PI/2, -0.2)
```

As you can see, the left/right actions rotate `GimbalOut` only on the *y* axis, while the up/down actions rotate `GimbalIn` on the *x* axis. The entire gimbal system's `scale` property is used to handle zooming. It is also necessary to set some limits using `clamp()`. The rotation limit holds up/down movement between `-0.2` (almost level with the ground) to `-90` degrees (looking straight down) while the zoom limit keeps you from getting too close or too far away.

Run the game and test the camera controls. You should be able to pan in all four directions and zoom with your mouse wheel. However, the gimbal's position is still static, so you may have trouble seeing the ball properly from certain angles.

Tracking camera

There is one final improvement to the camera: making it follow the ball. Now that you have a stable, gimbaled camera, it will work great if the gimbal is set to follow the ball's position. Add this line to the `Main` scene's `_process()` function:

```
$GimbalOut.transform.origin = $Ball.transform.origin
```

Note that you shouldn't set the gimbal's transform to the ball's transform, or it will also *rotate* as the ball rolls!

Try the game now and observe how the camera tracks the ball's movement while still being able to rotate and zoom.

Visual effects

The appearance of the ball and the other meshes in your scene have been intentionally left very plain. You can think of the flat, white ball like a blank canvas, ready to be molded and shaped the way you want it. Applying graphics to 3D models can be a very complex process, especially if you're not familiar with it. First, a bit of vocabulary:

- **Textures**: Textures are flat, 2D images that are *wrapped* around 3D objects to give them more interesting appearances. Imagine wrapping a present: the flat paper is folded around the package, conforming to its shape. Textures can be very simple or quite complex depending on the shape they are designed to be applied to. An example of a simple one would be a small pattern of bricks that can be repeated on a large wall object.

- **Shaders**: While textures determine *what* is drawn on an object's surface, shaders determine *how* it is drawn. Imagine that same brick wall. How would it look if it were wet? The mesh and the texture would still be the same, but the way the light reflects from it would be quite different. This is the function of shaders: to alter the appearance of an object without actually changing it. Shaders are typically written in a specialized programming language and can use a great deal of advanced math, the details of which are beyond the scope of this book. For many effects, writing your own shader is unavoidable. However, Godot provides an alternative method of creating a shader for your object that allows for a great deal of customization without diving into shader code: `ShaderMaterial`.

- **Materials**: Godot uses a computer graphics model called **Physically Based Rendering** (**PBR**). The goal of PBR is to render the surface of objects in a way that more accurately models the way light works in the real world. These affects are applied to meshes using the `Material` property. Materials are essentially containers for textures and shaders. Rather than apply them individually, they are contained in the material, which is then added to the object. The material's properties determine how the textures and shader effects are applied. Using Godot's built-in material properties, you can simulate a wide range of realistic (or stylized) real-world physical materials, such as stone, cloth, or metal. If the built-in properties aren't enough for your purposes, you can write your own shader code to add even more effects.

You can add a PBR material to a mesh using a `SpatialMaterial`.

SpatialMaterials

Click on the ball's `MeshInstance` and, under **Material**, select **New SpatialMaterial**, then click the new material. You will see a great number of parameters, far more than can be covered in this book. This section will focus on some of the most useful ones for making the ball look more appealing. You are encouraged to visit `http://docs.godotengine.org/en/3.0/tutorials/3d/spatial_material.html` for a full explanation of all the `SpatialMaterial` settings. To improve the look of the ball, try experimenting with these parameters:

- **Albedo**: This property sets the base color of the material. Change this to make the ball whatever color you like. If you're working with an object that needs a texture to be applied, you can add it here as well.

- **Metallic and Roughness**: These parameters control how reflective the surface is. Both can be set to values between 0 and 1. The Metallic value controls the *shininess*; higher values will reflect more light. The *Roughness* value applies an amount of blur to the reflection. You can simulate a wide variety of materials by adjusting these two properties. The following is a guide to how the *Roughness* and *Metallic* properties affect the appearance of an object. Keep in mind that lighting and other factors will alter the surface appearance as well. Understanding how light and reflections interact with surface properties is a big part of learning to design effective 3D objects:

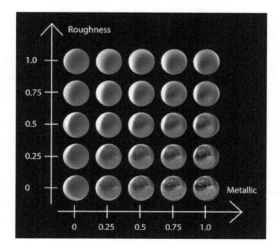

- **Normal Map**: Normal mapping is a 3D graphics technique for *faking* the appearance of bumps and dents in a surface. Modeling these in the mesh itself would result in a large increase in the number of polygons, or faces, making up the object, leading to reduced performance. Instead, a 2D texture is used that maps the pattern of light and shadow that would result from these small surface features. The lighting engine then uses that information to alter the lighting as if those details were actually there. A properly constructed normal map can add a great amount of detail to an otherwise bland-looking object.

The ball is a perfect example of a good use of normal mapping because a real golf ball has hundreds of dimples on its surface, but the sphere primitive is a smooth surface. Using a regular texture could add spots, but they would look flat and painted on. A normal map that would simulate those dimples looks like this:

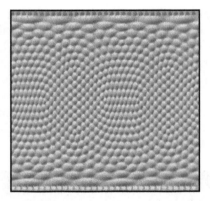

It doesn't look like much, but the pattern of red and blue contains information telling the engine which direction it should assume the surface is facing at that point and therefore which direction light should reflect from it there. Note the stretching along the top and the bottom—that's because this image is made to be wrapped around a sphere shape.

Enable the **Normal Map** property and drag `res://assets/ball_normal_map.png` into the *Texture* field. Try this with the *Albedo* color set to white at first, so you can best see the effect. Adjust the `Depth` parameter to increase or decrease the strength of the effect. A negative value will make the dimples look inset; something between `-1.0` and `-1.5` is a good value:

Take some time to experiment with these settings and find a combination you like. Don't forget to try it in the game as well, as the ambient lighting of the WorldEnvironment will effect the final result.

Environment options

When you added the WorldEnvironment, the only parameter you changed was the *Ambient Light* color. In this section, you'll learn about some of the other properties you can adjust for improved visual appeal:

- **Background**: This parameter lets you specify what the background of the world looks like. The default value is Clear Color, which is the plain grey you see currently. Change the **Mode** to **Sky** and, in the **Sky** property, choose **New Procedural Sky**. Note that the sky is not just for background appearance—objects will reflect and absorb its ambient light. Observe how the ball's appearance changes as you change the Energy parameter. This setting can be used to give the impression of a day or night sky, or even that of an alien planet.

- **Screen Space Ambient Occlusion (SSAO):** When enabled, this parameter works together with any ambient light to produce shadows in corners. You have two sources of ambient light now: the *Background* (sky) and the *Ambient Light* settings. Enable SSAO and you'll immediately see an improvement, making the walls of the course look much less fake and plastic. Feel free to try adjusting the various SSAO properties, but remember, a small change can make a big difference. Adjust the properties in small increments, and observe the effects before changing them further.

- **DOF Far Blur:** *Depth of Field* adds a blur effect to objects that are above a certain distance from the camera. Try adjusting the **Distance** property to see the effect.

For more information about advanced usage of environmental effects, see `http://docs.godotengine.org/en/3.0/tutorials/3d/environment_and_post_processing.html`.

Lighting

Add a `DirectionalLight` to the scene. This type of light simulates an infinite number of parallel rays of light, so it's often used to represent sunlight or another very distant source of light that illuminates an entire area equally. The location of the node in the scene doesn't matter, only its direction, so you can position it anywhere you like. Aim it using the gizmo so that it strikes the course at an angle, then turn **Shadow/Enabled** to **On** so that you'll see shadows being cast from the walls and other objects:

There are a number of properties available to adjust and alter the appearance of the shadows, both in the *Shadow* section, which is present for all `Light` nodes, and in the *Directional Shadow* section, which is specific to `DirectionalLight`. The default values will work for most general cases, but the one property that you should probably adjust to improve shadow appearance is *Max Distance*. Lowering this value will improve shadow appearance, but only when the camera is closer than the given distance. If your camera will mostly be close to objects, you can reduce this value. To see the effect, try setting it to just `10` and zooming in/out, then do the same with it set to `1000`.

Directional light can even be used to simulate the day/night cycle. If you attach a script to the light and slowly rotate it around one axis, you'll see the shadows change as if the sun is rising and setting.

Summary

This chapter introduced you to the world of 3D graphics. One of Godot's great strengths is that the same tools and workflow are used in both 2D and 3D. Everything you learned about the process of creating scenes, instancing, and using signals works in the same way. For example, an interface you build with control nodes for a 2D game can be dropped into a 3D game and will work just the same.

In this chapter, you learned how to navigate in the the 3D editor to view and place nodes using gizmos. You learned about meshes and how to quickly make your own objects using Godot's primitives. You used GridMap to lay out your minigolf course. You learned about using cameras, lighting, and the world environment to design how your game will appear on screen. Finally, you got a taste of using PBR rendering via Godot's SpatialMaterial resource.

Congratulations, you've made it to the end! But with these five projects, your journey to becoming a game developer has just begun. As you become more proficient with Godot's features, you'll be able to make any game you can imagine.

Additional Topics 7

Congratulations! The projects you've built in this book have started you on the road to becoming a Godot expert. However, you've only just scratched the surface of what's possible in Godot. As you become more proficient, and the size of your projects grows, you'll need to know how to find solutions to your problems, how to distribute your games so they can be played, and even how to extend the engine yourself.

In this chapter, you'll learn about the following topics:

- How to effectively use Godot's built-in documentation
- Exporting projects to run on other platforms
- Using other programming languages in Godot
- How to use Godot's asset library to install plugins
- Becoming a Godot contributor
- Community resources

Using Godot's documentation

Learning Godot's API can seem overwhelming at first. How can you learn all the different nodes, and the properties and methods each one contains? Fortunately, Godot's built-in documentation is there to help you. Develop the habit of using it often: it will help you find things when you're learning, but it's also a great way to quickly look up a method or property for reference once you know your way around.

When you are in the **Script** tab of the editor, you'll see the following buttons in the upper-right corner:

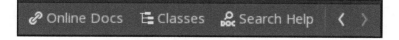

The **Online Docs** button will open the documentation website in your browser. If you have a multimonitor setup, it can be very useful to keep the API reference open on one side for quick reference while you're working in Godot.

The other two buttons allow you to view the documentation directly in the Godot editor. The **Classes** button allows you to browse through the available node and object types, while the **Search Help** button lets you search for any method or property name. Both searches are *smart*, meaning you can type part of a word and the results will be narrowed down as you type. Take a look at the following screenshot:

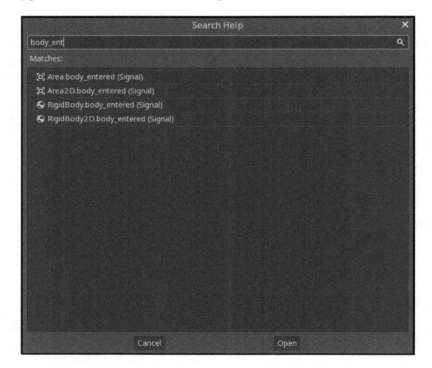

When you find the property or method you're looking for, click **Open** and the documentation reference for that node will appear.

Reading the API documentation

When you've found the documentation for the node you want, you'll see that it follows a common format, with the name of the node at the top followed by several subsections of information, as shown in the following screenshot:

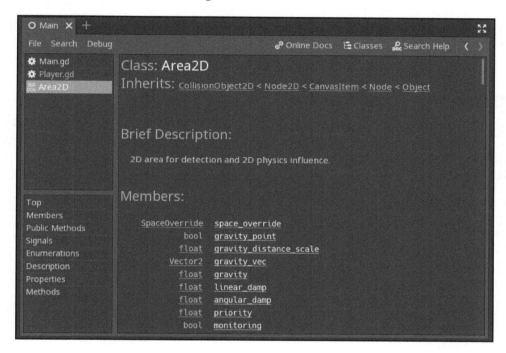

At the top of the document is a list titled **Inherits**, which shows you the chain of classes that a particular node is built from all the way back to `Object`, which is Godot's base object class. For example, an `Area2D` node has the following inheritance chain:

```
CollisionObject2D < Node2D < CanvasItem < Node < Object
```

This lets you quickly see what other properties this type of object may have. You can click on any of the node names to jump to that node's documentation.

You can also see a list of what node types, if any, inherit from that particular node, as well as a general description of the node. Below that, you can see the member variables and methods of the node. The names of most methods and types are links, so you can click on any item to read more about it.

Develop the habit of consulting the API documentation regularly as you work. You'll find that you will quickly begin to develop a stronger understanding of how everything works together.

Exporting projects

Eventually, your project will reach the stage where you want to share it with the world. *Exporting* your project means converting it into a package that can be run by someone who doesn't have the Godot editor. You can export your project for a number of popular platforms.

At the time of writing, Godot supports the following target platforms:

- Windows Universal
- Windows Desktop
- macOS
- Linux
- Android (mobile)
- iOS (mobile)
- HTML5 (web)

The method for exporting the project varies depending on the platform you are targeting. For example, to export for iOS, you must be running on a macOS computer with Xcode installed.

Each platform is unique, and some features of your game may not work on some platforms because of hardware limitations, screen size, or other factors. As an example, if you wanted to export the Coin Dash game (from `Chapter 1`, *Introduction*) for the Android platform, your player wouldn't be able to move because the keyboard controls wouldn't work! For that platform, you would need to include touchscreen controls in your game's code (more about this later).

You may even find that you need to set different values in **Project Settings** for different platforms. You can do this by selecting the setting and clicking **Override For....**This will create a new setting specific to that platform.

For example, if you want to enable HiDPI support, but not allow it for Android, you can create an override for that setting:

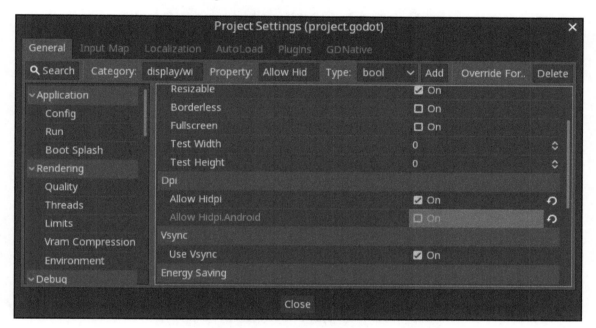

 Every platform is unique, and there are many factors to consider when configuring your project for export. Consult the official documentation for the latest instructions on exporting to your desired platform.

Getting the export templates

Export templates are versions of Godot that are compiled for each target platform, but don't include the editor. Your project will be combined with the target platform's template to create a standalone application.

To begin, you must download the export templates. Click on **Manage Export Templates** from the **Editor** menu:

In this window, you can click **Download** to fetch the export templates:

Templates can also be downloaded from the Godot website at `http://godotengine.org/download`. If you choose to do this, use the **Install From File** button to complete the installation.

The template's version must match the version of Godot you are using. If you upgrade to a new version of Godot, make sure that you also download the corresponding templates, or your exported project may not work properly.

Export presets

When you're ready to export your project, click on **Project** | **Export**:

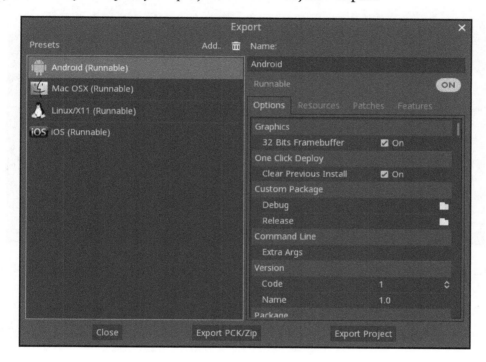

In this window, you can create *presets* for each platform by clicking **Add...** and selecting the platform from the list. You can make as many presets for each platform as you wish. For example, you may want to create both **Debug** and **Release** versions of your projects.

Each platform has its own settings and options, too many to describe here. The default values are typically good, but you should test them thoroughly before distributing the project.

In the **Resources** tab, you can customize which portions of your project are exported. For example, you can choose to only export selected scenes or to exclude certain source files from the project:

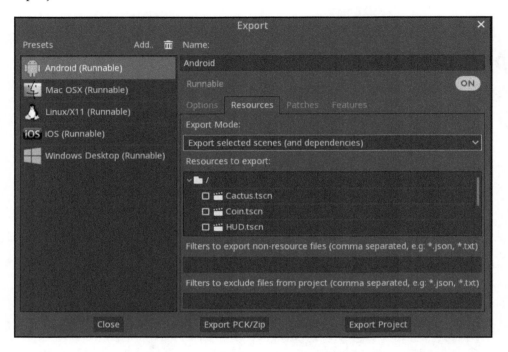

The **Patches** tab allows you to create updates for your previously exported projects.

Finally, the **Features** tab displays a summary of the features (configured in the **Options** tab) for the platform. These features can determine which properties are customized by the **Override** value in the **Project Settings**:

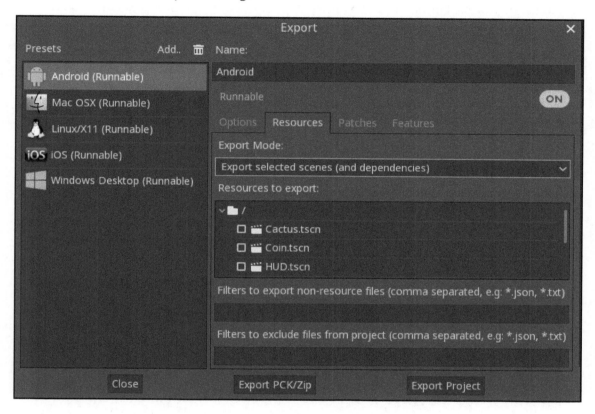

Exporting

There are two export buttons at the bottom of the window. The first button, **Export PCK/Zip**, will only create a PCK, or packed, version of your project's data. This doesn't include an executable, so the game can't be run on its own. This method is useful if you need to provide add-ons or DLC (downloadable content) for your game.

The second button, **Export Project**, will create an executable version of your game, such as an .exe for Windows or an .apk for Android.

Click **Save** and you will have a playable version of your game.

Example – Coin Dash for Android

If you have an Android device, you can follow this example to export the Coin Dash game for mobile platforms. For other platforms, see Godot's documentation at `http://docs.` `godotengine.org/en/latest/getting_started/workflow/export`.

Mobile devices come with a wide variety of capabilities. Always consult the official documentation in the preceding link for information on your platform and what restrictions, if any, may apply to your device. In most cases, Godot's default settings will work, but mobile development is sometimes more art than science, and you may need to do some experimenting and searching for help in order to get everything working.

Modifying the game

Because the game as written in this chapter uses keyboard controls, you won't be able to play on a mobile device without making some changes. Fortunately, Godot has support for touchscreen input. First, open **Project Settings**, and in the **Display/Window** section, make sure **Orientation** is set to **portrait** and **Emulate Touchscreen** is **On**. This will let you test the program on your computer by treating mouse clicks as touch events:

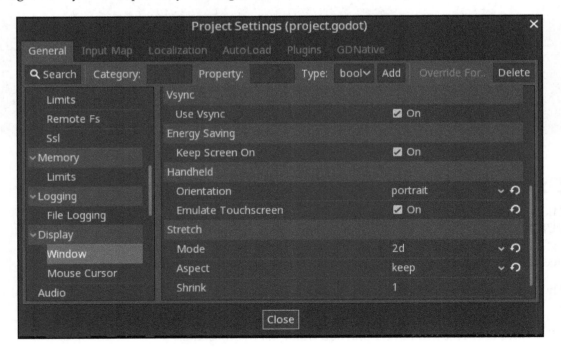

Next, you need to change the player controls. Instead of using the four direction inputs, the player will move toward the position of the touch event. Change the player script as follows:

```
var target = Vector2()

func _input(event):
    if event is InputEventScreenTouch and event.pressed:
        target = event.position

func _process(delta):
    velocity = (target - position).normalized() * speed
    if (target - position).length() > 5:
        position += velocity * delta
    else:
        velocity = Vector2()

    if velocity.length() > 0:
        $AnimatedSprite.animation = "run"
        $AnimatedSprite.flip_h = velocity.x < 0
    else:
        $AnimatedSprite.animation = "idle"
```

Try it out and make sure that mouse clicks are causing the player to move. If everything is working, you're ready to set up your computer for Android development.

Preparing your system

In order to export your project to Android, you'll need to download the Android **software development kit (SDK)** from https://developer.android.com/studio/ and the **Java Development Kit (JDK)** from http://www.oracle.com/technetwork/java/javase/downloads/index.html.

When you run Android Studio for the first time, click on **Configure | SDK Manager** and make sure that you install **Android SDK Platform-Tools**:

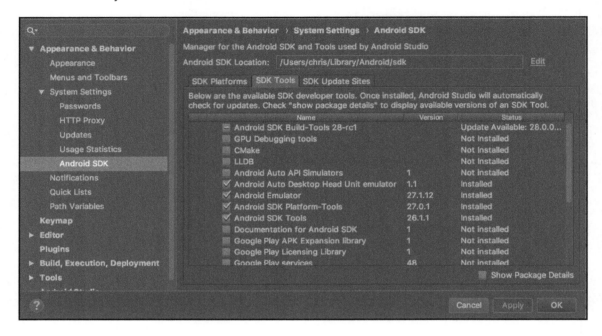

This will install the `adb` command-line tool, which Godot uses to communicate with your device.

After you've installed the development tools, create a debug keystore by running the following command:

```
keytool -keyalg RSA -genkeypair -alias androiddebugkey -keypass android -
keystore debug.keystore -storepass android -dname "CN=Android
Debug,O=Android,C=US" -validity 9999
```

In Godot, click on **Editor | Editor Settings**, find the **Export/Android** section, and set the paths to the applications on your system. Note that you'll only have to do this once, as the editor settings are independent of the project settings:

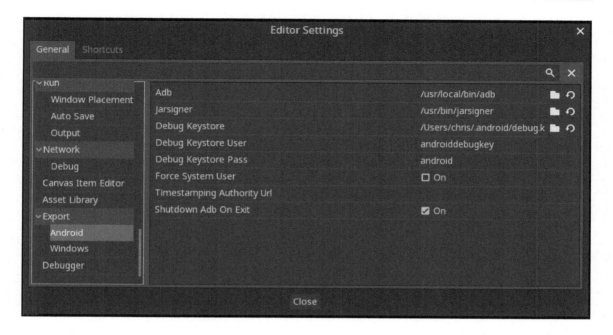

Exporting

You're now ready to export. Click on **Project | Export** and add a preset for Android (see the previous section). Click the **Export Project** button and you'll have an **Android Package Kit** (**APK**) you can install on your device. You can do this with a graphical tool or from the command line using `adb`:

```
adb install dodge.apk
```

Note that if your system supports it, connecting a compatible Android device will cause the one-click deploy button to appear in the Godot editor:

Clicking this button will export the project and install it on your device in one step. Your device may need to be in developer mode for this to happen: consult your device's documentation for details.

Shaders

A *shader* is a program that is designed to run in the GPU, and alters the way that objects appear on the screen. Shaders are used extensively in both 2D and 3D development to create a variety of visual effects. They are called shaders because they were originally used for shading and lighting effects, but today they are used for any number of visual effects. Because they run in the GPU in *parallel*, they are very fast, but also come with some restrictions.

 This section is a very brief introduction to the concept of shaders. For a more in-depth understanding, see `https://thebookofshaders.com/` and Godot's shader documentation at `http://docs.godotengine.org/en/ latest/tutorials/shading/shading_language.html`.

In Godot 3.0, shaders are written in a language very similar to GLSL ES 3.0. If you are familiar with C, you will find the syntax very similar. If you are not, it may look strange to you at first. See the end of this section for links to further resources where you can learn more.

Shaders in Godot come in three types: **spatial** (for 3D rendering), **canvas item** (for 2D), and **particles** (for rendering particle effects). The first line of your shader must declare which of these types you are writing.

After determining the type of shader, you have another three choices of what render phase(s) you want to affect: fragment, vertex, and/or light. Fragment shaders are used to set the color of every affected pixel. Vertex shaders are used to modify the vertices of a shape or mesh (and thus are typically used more in 3D applications). Finally, light shaders are applied to alter the way light is processed for an object.

After choosing the type(s) of your shader, you will then write code that will be run *simultaneously* on every affected item. This is where the real power of shaders comes from. For example, when using a fragment shader, the code is run on every pixel of the object at the same time. This is a very different process than what you might be used to using a traditional language, where you would loop over each pixel one at a time. That kind of sequential code just isn't fast enough to handle the huge number of pixels modern games need to process.

 Consider a game running at the relatively low resolution of 480 x 720. The total number of pixels on the screen is almost 350,000. Any manipulation of those pixels in code must happen in less than 1/60 of a second to avoid lag—even less when you consider the rest of your code that also has to run for every frame: game logic, animation, networking, and everything else. This is why GPUs are so important, especially for high-end games that may be processing millions of pixels for each frame.

Creating a shader

To demonstrate some shader effects, create a scene with a `Sprite` node and choose any texture you like. This demo will use the cactus image from Coin Dash:

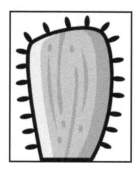

A shader can be added to any `CanvasItem` derived node—in this case, `Sprite`, via its **Material** property. In this property, select **New Shader Material** and click on the newly created resource. The first property is **Shader**, where you can choose a **New Shader**. When you do, a **Shader** panel appears at the bottom of the editor window.

This is where you'll write your shader code:

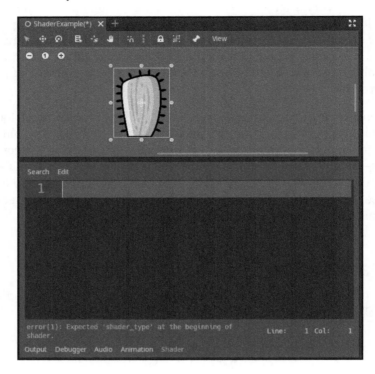

A blank shader looks like the following:

```
shader_type canvas_item; // choose spatial, canvas_item, or particles

void fragment(){
    // code in this function runs on every pixel
}

void vertex() {
    // code in this function runs on each vertex
}

void light() {
    // code in this function affects light processing
}
```

For the purposes of this example, you'll be coding a 2D-fragment shader, so you won't need to include the other two functions.

Shader functions have a number of *built-ins*, which are either input values or output values. For example, the TEXTURE input built-in contains the pixel data of the object's texture, while the COLOR output built-in is used to set the result of your calculation. Remember, a fragment shader's purpose is to affect the color of every processed pixel.

When working with shaders in the TEXTURE property, for example, coordinates are measured in a *normalized* (that is, ranging from 0 to 1) coordinate space. This coordinate space is called UV to distinguish it from the *x/y* coordinate space:

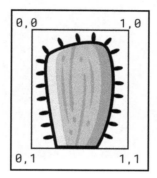

As a result, all values in coordinate vectors will range from 0 and 1.

As a very small example, this first shader will take the pixels of the cactus image and change them all to a single color. To allow you to choose the color, you can use a uniform variable.

Uniforms allow you to pass data into the shader from outside. Declaring a uniform variable will cause it to appear in the **Inspector** (similar to how export works in GDScript) and also allow you to set it via code.

Type the following code into the **Shader** panel:

```
shader_type canvas_item;

uniform vec4 fill_color:hint_color;

void fragment(){
    COLOR.rgb = fill_color.rgb;
}
```

You should see the image change immediately: The whole image turns black. To select a different color, click on the **Material** in the inspector, and you'll see your uniform variable listed under **Shader Param**:

You're not done, however. The image just turned to a colored rectangle, but you only want the cactus to change color, not its surrounding transparent pixels. Add one more line after setting COLOR.rgb:

```
COLOR.a = texture(TEXTURE, UV).a;
```

This last line makes the shader output every pixel with the same alpha (transparency) value as the pixel in the original texture. Now the empty area around the cactus remains transparent, with an alpha of 0.

The following code shows one more example. In this shader, you create a blur effect by setting each pixel's color to the average value of the pixels around it:

```
shader_type canvas_item;

uniform float radius = 10.0;

void fragment(){
    vec4 new_color = texture(TEXTURE, UV);
    vec2 pixel_size = TEXTURE_PIXEL_SIZE; // size of the texture in pixels

    new_color += texture(TEXTURE, UV + vec2(0, -radius) * pixel_size);
    new_color += texture(TEXTURE, UV + vec2(0, radius) * pixel_size);
    new_color += texture(TEXTURE, UV + vec2(-radius, 0) * pixel_size);
```

```
    new_color += texture(TEXTURE, UV + vec2(radius, 0) * pixel_size);

    COLOR = new_color / 5.0;
}
```

Note that since you've added five color values together (the original pixel's, plus the four that are found by moving in each direction around it), you need to divide by 5.0 to get the average value. The larger you make the radius, the more "smeared" the image looks:

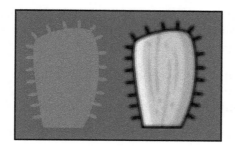

Learning more

Shaders are capable of an amazing range of effects. Experimenting with Godot's shader language is a great way to learn the basics, but there is also a wealth of resources on the internet for learning more. When learning about shaders, you can use resources that aren't specific to Godot, and you shouldn't have much trouble getting them to work in Godot. The concept is the same across all types of graphics applications.

To see some examples of just how powerful shaders can be, visit https://www.shadertoy.com/.

Using other languages

The projects in this book have all been written using GDScript. GDScript has a number of advantages that make it the best choice for building your games. It is very tightly integrated with Godot's API, and its Python-style syntax makes it useful for rapid development while also being very beginner-friendly.

It's not the only option, however. Godot also supports two other "official" scripting languages, and also provides tools for integrating code using a variety of other languages.

C#

With the release of Godot 3.0 in early 2018, support was added for C# as a scripting language for the first time. C# is very popular in game development, and the Godot version is based on the Mono 5.2 .NET framework. Because of its wide use, there are many resources available for learning C# and a great deal of existing code in the language for accomplishing a variety of game-related functions.

At the time of writing, the current Godot version is 3.0.2. In this version, C# support should be considered preliminary; it is functional, but has not been fully tested. Some features and capabilities, such as exporting projects, are not yet supported.

If you want to try out the C# implementation, you'll need to first make sure you have Mono installed, which you can get from `http://www.mono-project.com/download/`. You must also download the Godot version that has C# support included, which you can find at `http://godotengine.org/download` where it is labeled **Mono Version**.

You'll probably also want to use an external editor—such as Visual Studio Code or MonoDevelop—that provides more debugging and language functionality than Godot's built-in editor. You can set this in **Editor Settings** under the **Mono** section.

To attach a C# script to a node, select the language from the **Attach Node Script** dialog:

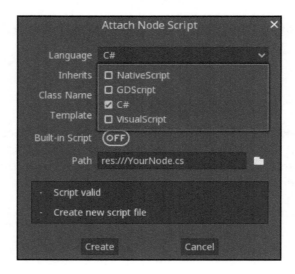

In general, scripting in C# works very much the same as what you've seen with GDScript. The main difference is that API functions are renamed in `PascalCase` to follow C# standards instead of `snake_case`, which is the standard for GDScript.

Here is an example of `KinematicBody2D` movement using C#:

```csharp
using Godot;
using System;

public class Movement : KinematicBody2D
{
    [Export] public int speed = 200;

    Vector2 velocity = new Vector2();

    public void GetInput()
    {
        velocity = new Vector2();
        if (Input.IsActionPressed("right"))
        {
            velocity.x += 1;
        }
        if (Input.IsActionPressed("left"))
        {
            velocity.x -= 1;
        }
        if (Input.IsActionPressed("down"))
        {
            velocity.y += 1;
        }
        if (Input.IsActionPressed("up"))
        {
            velocity.y -= 1;
        }
        velocity = velocity.Normalized() * speed;
    }

    public override void _PhysicsProcess(float delta)
    {
        GetInput();
        MoveAndSlide(velocity);
    }
}
```

For more details about using C#, see the **Scripting** section of the documentation at `http://docs.godotengine.org/en/latest/getting_started/scripting/`.

VisualScript

Visual scripting is intended to provide an alternative scripting method using a drag-and-drop visual metaphor instead of written code. To create a script, you drag nodes (not to be confused with Godot's nodes) representing functions and data, and connect them by drawing lines. Running your script means following the path of the line through the nodes. The goal of this style of presentation is to provide a more intuitive way to visualize program flow for non-programmers, such as artists or animators, who need to collaborate on a project.

In practice, this goal has yet to be reached in a practical way. Godot's VisualScript was also added for the first time in version 3.0, and it is currently not mature enough as a feature to be used in an actual project. As with C#, it should be considered in testing, and if you're interested in it, your testing and feedback will be very valuable to the Godot team in improving its functionality.

One potential strength of VisualScript is to use it as a second layer of scripting. You can create an object's core behavior in GDScript, and then a game designer can use a VisualScript that calls the functions of those scripts in visual nodes.

The following screenshot is an example VisualScript project. Here, you can see a portion of the player movement code in Coin Dash:

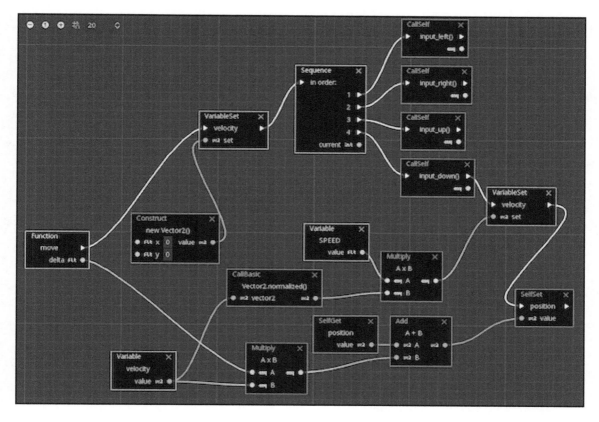

The player movement code in Coin Dash

Native code – GDNative

There are many programming languages to choose from. Each has its strengths and weaknesses, as well as its fans who prefer to use it over other options. While it doesn't make sense to support every language directly in Godot, there are situations where GDScript is no longer sufficient to solve a particular problem. Perhaps you want to use an existing external library, or you're doing something computationally intensive—such as AI or procedural world generation—that doesn't make sense for GDScript.

Because GDScript is an interpreted language, it trades performance for flexibility. This means that for some processor-intensive code, it can run unacceptably slow. In this case, the highest performance would be achieved by running native code written in a compiled language. In this situation, you can move that code to a GDNative library.

GDNative is a C API that can be used by external libraries to interface with Godot. These external libraries can be your own or any existing third-party libraries that you may need for a particular project.

In GDScript, you can then use the GDNative and GDNativeLibrary classes to load and call functions from these libraries. The following code is an example of calling a library that has been saved as a GDNativeLibrary resource file:

```
extends Node

func _ready():
    var lib = GDNative.new()
    lib.library = load("res://somelib.tres")
    lib.initialize()

    // call functions in the library
    var result = lib.call_native("call_type", "some_function",
arguments_array)

    lib.terminate()
```

Whereas, the library might look something like this (in C):

```
#include <gdnative.h>

void GDN_EXPORT godot_gdnative_init(godot_gdnative_init_options *p_options)
{
    // initialization code
}

void GDN_EXPORT godot_gdnative_terminate(godot_gdnative_terminate_options
*p_options) {
    // termination code
}

void GDN_EXPORT godot_nativescript_init(void *p_handle) {
}

godot_variant GDN_EXPORT some_function(void *args) {
    // Do something
}
```

Keep in mind that writing code like this is definitely more involved than sticking to pure GDScript. In a native language, you'll need to handle calling constructors and destructors for objects and manually manage working with Godot's `Variant` class. You should only resort to using GDNative when performance truly becomes an issue, and even then, only use it if the functionality really demands its use.

If this section made no sense at all to you, don't worry. Most Godot developers will never need to delve into this side of development. Even if you find yourself needing higher-performance code, you may only need to look at the Asset library to find that someone has already created a library for you. You can find out about the Asset library in the next section.

Language bindings

Another benefit of GDNative is that it has allowed proponents of other languages to create API bindings to enable scripting in those languages.

At the time of writing, several projects are available that use GDNative to allow you to use other languages for scripting. These include C, C++, Python, Nim, D, Go, and others. While these additional language bindings are still relatively new at the time of writing, they each have a dedicated group of developers working on them. If you're interested in using a particular language with Godot, a Google search of "godot + <language name>" will help you find what's available.

Asset library

At the top of the editor window, in the **Workspaces** section, you'll find a button labeled **AssetLib**:

Clicking this button will take you to Godot's Asset library. This is a collection of add-ons, tools, and utilities contributed by the Godot community that you may find useful in your projects. For example, if you search for `State`, you'll see that there is a tool called **finite state machine** (**FSM**) available in the library. You can click on its name for more information, and if you decide you want to try it out, click **Install** to download it into the `res://addons/` folder, which will be created if it doesn't already exist:

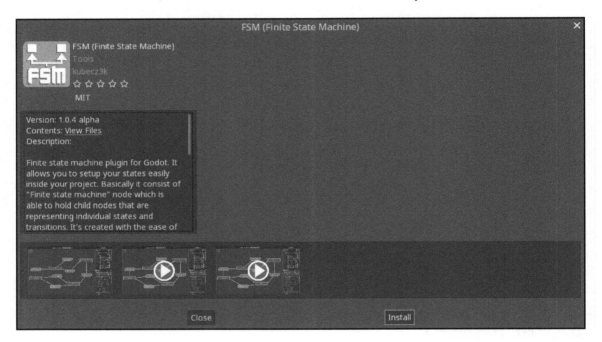

You then need to enable the add-on by opening **Project Settings** and choosing the **Plugins** tab:

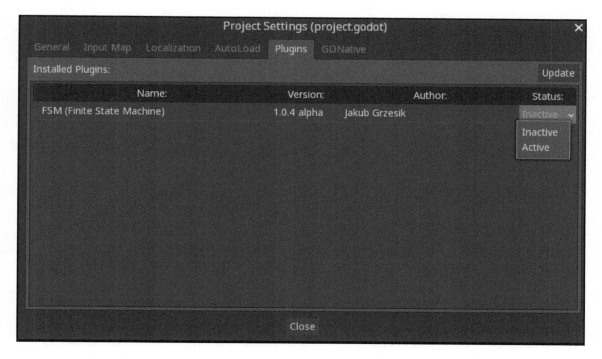

The plugin is now ready to use. Be sure to read the plugin author's instructions to understand how it works.

Contributing to Godot

Godot is an open source, community-driven project. All of the work that's done to build, test, document, and otherwise support Godot is done primarily by passionate individuals contributing their time and skills. For the majority of contributors, it is a labor of love, and they take pride in helping to build something of quality that people enjoy using.

In order for Godot to continue growing and improving, there is always a need for more members of the community to step up and contribute. There are many ways you can help out, regardless of your skill level or the amount of time you can commit.

Contributing to the engine

There are two main ways you can directly contribute to Godot's development. If you visit `https://github.com/godotengine/godot`, you can see Godot's source code, as well as find out exactly what's being worked on. Click the **Clone or Download** button, and you'll have the up-to-the-minute source code and can test out the latest features. You'll need to build the engine, but don't be intimidated: Godot is one of the easiest open source projects to compile that you'll find. See `http://docs.godotengine.org/en/latest/development/compiling/` for instructions.

If you're not able to actually contribute to the C++ code, go to the **Issues** tab, where you can report or read about bugs and suggestions for improvements. There is always a need for people to confirm bug reports, test fixes, and give their opinions on new features.

Writing documentation

Godot's official documentation is only as good as its community's contributions. From something as small as correcting a typo to writing an entire tutorial, all levels of help are very welcome. The home of the official documentatin is `https://github.com/godotengine/godot-docs`.

Hopefully, by now you've taken some time to browse through the official documentation and get an idea of what's available. If you spot something wrong or something missing, open an issue at the aforementioned GitHub link. If you're comfortable with using GitHub, you can even go ahead and submit a pull request yourself. Just make sure you read all the guidelines first so that your contribution will be accepted. You can find the guidelines at `http://docs.godotengine.org/en/latest/community/contributing/`.

 If you speak a language other than English, translations are also very much needed, and will be greatly appreciated by Godot's non-English-speaking users. See `https://hosted.weblate.org/projects/godot-engine/godot-docs/` for how to contribute in your language.

Donations

Godot is a not-for-profit project, and user donations go a long way to help pay for hosting costs and development resources, such as hardware. Financial contributions also allow the project to pay core developers, allowing them to dedicate themselves part- or full-time to working on the engine.

The easiest way to contribute to Godot is via the Patreon page at `https://www.patreon.com/godotengine`.

Getting help – community resources

Godot's online community is one of its strengths. Because of its open source nature, there is a wide variety of people working together to improve the engine, write documentation, and help each other with issues.

You can find a full list of community resources at `https://godotengine.org/community`.

These links may change over time, but the following are the main community resources you should be aware of.

GitHub

`https://github.com/godotengine/`

The Godot GitHub repository is where Godot's developers work. You can find Godot's source code here, if you find yourself needing to compile a custom version of the engine for your own use.

If you find any kind of problem with the engine itself—something that doesn't work, a typo in the documentation, and so on—this is the place where you should report it.

Godot Q and A

`https://godotengine.org/qa/`

This is Godot's official help site. You can post questions here for the community to answer, as well as search the growing database of previously answered questions. If you happen to see a question you know the answer to, you can help out as well.

Discord / Forum

```
https://discord.gg/zH7NUgz
```

```
http://godotdevelopers.org/
```

While not *official*, these are two very active communities of Godot users where you can get help, find answers to questions, and discuss your project with others.

Summary

In this chapter, you learned about a few additional topics that will help you continue to level up your Godot skills. Godot has a great many features in addition to those explored in this book. You'll need to know where to look and where to ask for help as you move on to working on projects of your own.

You also learned about some more advanced topics, such as working with other programming languages and using shaders to enhance your game's visual effects.

In addition, since Godot is built by its community, you learned how you can participate and become part of the team that is making it one of the fastest-growing projects of its kind.

Other Books You May Enjoy

If you enjoyed this book, you may be interested in these other books by Packt:

Getting Started with Unity 2018 - Third Edition
Dr. Edward Lavieri

ISBN: 9781788830102

- Set up your Unity development environment and navigate its tools
- Import and use custom assets and asset packages to add characters to your game
- Build a 3D game world with a custom terrain, water, sky, mountains, and trees
- Animate game characters, using animation controllers, and scripting
- Apply audio and particle effects to the game
- Create intuitive game menus and interface elements
- Customize your game with sound effects, shadows, lighting effects, and rendering options
- Debug code and provide smooth error handling

Unity Virtual Reality Projects - Second Edition
Jonathan Linowes

ISBN: 9781788478809

- Create 3D scenes with Unity and other 3D tools while learning about world space and scale
- Build and run VR applications for specific headsets, including Oculus, Vive, and Daydream
- Interact with virtual objects using eye gaze, hand controllers, and user input events
- Move around your VR scenes using locomotion and teleportation
- Implement an audio fireball game using physics and particle systems
- Implement an art gallery tour with teleportation and data info
- Design and build a VR storytelling animation with a soundtrack and timelines
- Create social VR experiences with Unity networking

Leave a review - let other readers know what you think

Please share your thoughts on this book with others by leaving a review on the site that you bought it from. If you purchased the book from Amazon, please leave us an honest review on this book's Amazon page. This is vital so that other potential readers can see and use your unbiased opinion to make purchasing decisions, we can understand what our customers think about our products, and our authors can see your feedback on the title that they have worked with Packt to create. It will only take a few minutes of your time, but is valuable to other potential customers, our authors, and Packt. Thank you!

Index

V